Accommodating and Educating

SOMALI STUDENTS

in Minnesota Schools

A Handbook for Teachers and Administrators

Mohamed Farid | Don McMahan

Hamline University Press
Saint Paul, Minnesota
2004

Hamline University
1536 Hewitt Avenue
Saint Paul, Minnesota 55104-1284
Copyright © 2004 by Hamline University. All rights reserved.
ISBN 0-9723721-4-8
Library of Congress Control Number 2004113536

Book editing, design, layout, and production management by Carr Creatives
First printing 2004
Printed in U.S.A.

PREFACE

The question our handbook addresses is complex: What information will help public school teachers and administrators accommodate and educate Somali students? This handbook was a collaborative effort that grew out of shared commitments and values. We are ESL/ELL teachers who are committed to increased cultural understanding and good education of young people whose first language is not English.

We developed this handbook to fulfill the thesis requirement for the Master of Arts in Education degree at Hamline University, Saint Paul, Minnesota. Our collaboration continues as we seek to share this information widely with teachers and administrators, to provide them with a scaffold to understand their Somali students, with a particular focus on helping students to adjust to, and be successful in, the peculiar culture of American public schools.

July, 2004   M.F.
Saint Paul, Minnesota   D.M.

THE AUTHORS:
MOHAMED FARID'S STORY

As an educator and new Somali immigrant, I believe that identifying what Minnesota educators need to know about the Somali students is a duty to be shared by Somali educators. My personal story in connection with the civil war in Somalia is a demonstration of some of the events that forced Somalis to immigrate to Minnesota and other parts of the world.

The experiences I went through with my own children while establishing their safety and future in the world have had a great impact on me. It led me, as a parent, an educator, and a responsible member of Minnesota's Somali community to believe that it is a noble calling to work with these children in need. It inspired my decision to develop a guide for Minnesota educators that could serve as a bridge between the Somali students and the Minnesota schools they attend.

December 19, 1990, is a date that I recall whenever I think of Somalia and the Somalis: It was my last evening in my home country of Somalia. I was beginning a trip of no return. Late that evening I was heading for a business trip to Nepal, India, and Thailand. Unlike the other trips I made out of Somalia, this time my wife and all my children accompanied me to Mogadishu Airport. Many of my personal friends and some of my relatives also came to say farewell. This kind of gathering at the airport on my departure for a business trip had never happened before. I sensed that the farewell would last for many years; a long period of separation from my family and friends was ahead.

My feeling toward the gathering was manageable compared to the touching words of my children while at the airport. I will always live with the meaningful words and the predictions of my oldest son, who repeatedly asked me, "When are you coming back from this trip, Dad? Come soon, we need you to be with us, Dad." At 15 years of age, my oldest son was mature enough to comprehend and predict some of the political trends and security matters in Mogadishu. The words of my six-year-old daughter made me feel guilty. As we were waiting at the airport, she came to me and kissed me and said, "Dad, this place is not a good place. It is not safe. Why don't we all move to where my grand-mother traveled a week before? That is a safer place."

Two weeks earlier, my mother had left Mogadishu and returned to Boramo, her hometown in the northern part of Somalia. In spite of my great love for my mother and my wish that she would stay with me in Mogadishu, I rushed to make arrangements for her flight to Boramo.

Several years earlier in Hargeisa, the capital city in the northern part of Somalia, I learned to be very serious about my mother's premo-nitions. On May 22, 1988, my mother and sister came from Jibouti, a small country neighboring Somalia and the home of my sister and her children, to visit me in Hargeisa. When I first met my mother that day, she said, "Hargeisa is not a safe place and I came to advise you and the family to move to Boramo immediately." I did not take her advice seri-ously. To my surprise, five days later, on May 27, 1988, at 2.30 a.m. Hargeisa was in flames. The whole city fell under the crossfire between government and opposing clan forces that were both brutal and cata-strophic for the children, the women, the old, and all the unarmed innocent civilians. This has brought disaster and destruction to a flour-ishing and heavily populated city.

That night at 2.30 a.m. was one of the moments in my life that I will never forget. The events around my house that night taught me a lesson on how parents respond to such perilous situations. I learned how parents feel when the lives of their children are at risk. I saw my mother, who forgot about herself and her safety, and thought only about my safety. I experienced the same feeling. I forgot everything else except how to protect and find a safe place for my children. It is impos-sible to describe in words the picture around my home that night, the shelling, the shooting, and the horrors of a civil war that created chaos and forced friends and neighbors to take sides in the conflict and begin killing each other. As the shelling eased a bit at 3.00 p.m. that day, I decided to go out and look for information of what was happening. It was horrible to see dead bodies in every street I passed by. I learned that in a civil war, you do not know who is the enemy and who is not, so it was also extremely dangerous that anyone seen walking or driving was a target. My house was a target, because I was managing money. I was lucky to move my family safely to a house of a relative close to my home.

Later, I sought possibilities to send my children to Mogadishu. Driving to the airport carried great risk, however. I decided to go anyway and was so lucky to meet the captain of the only military plane, who happened to be a friend of mine. It was rather a miracle to see my children on that flight to Mogadishu. I always thank to Allah (God) who gave me that opportunity, and I felt sad for those children and their parents who could not make the trip and were forced to risk driving back.

The memories of my experiences in Hargeisa added fuel to the fire during my flight back from the business trip to the Far East. On December 30, 1990, the CNN news reported the civil war in Mogadishu as I came back to my hotel in New Delhi, India. My attempts to call my family became impossible, and I rushed to find the earliest flight to Cairo, my only possible air route to Somalia. As the Gulfair hostess seated me, I could not wait to ask for the Gulf daily newspaper in Arabic, which I thought could carry more information on the situation in Somalia. As I read the articles on Somalia and their analysis, the memories of the horrors in Hargeisa rushed into my mind, and I saw myself thinking over the worst scenarios that my loved ones, especially my children, could go through. It was one of my hardest moments as parent, to know my children, families and friends and country were under the mercy of the worst civil war in Somalia's modern history.

I felt better when experiencing the situation in Hargeisa, as if I was there feeling the fear and the pain with my family, instead of being alone, outside my country, knowing nothing about the situation and thinking of worst scenarios. I did not know if the flight from Delhi to Cairo took a minute or ten hours. I was only physically there. However, when the flight ended at Cairo airport, I rushed to find information on flights to Mogadishu, but to no avail. The last flight left Cairo the day before and I had no other choice but to stay in Cairo and look for family information.

After spending few nights in Cairo and getting no news from my children, the Gulf War started and the situation became worse. Commercial airlines stopped their flights in that area of the world, and I was stuck in Cairo. It took three months to get the first news that my children and my wife were alive and had fled to Kenya. I managed to bring them to Cairo after one more month.

We spent almost two and half years there. During this time as a parent, my focus and thinking was to appraise and evaluate the possibilities of going back to my country, but the hopes of this dream quickly began to fade. The priorities in my mind and the focus of my efforts were to find a safe place and to be able to feed my family. The responsibilities of parenting my kids and teaching them their cultural values and thinking of their education became a luxury. Compared to other Somali parents, mostly single mothers who went with their children to the refugee camps, my children had parental care and were better educated to some degree. As time went on, our hope to go back to Somalia faded. I began to look for a safe place to settle in the world. I will never forget the wonderful face of a young woman in the American Embassy in Cairo who welcomed me warmly and helped us to immigrate to the United States. My kids started school less than a week after our arrival on February 16, 1993. As a parent I instantly started to think about my kids and their education and how they could adjust in the new environment.

I am writing about my personal experiences because I am trying to describe certain events of my history as an introduction to this handbook in order to demonstrate that most of the experiences that Somali Students in Minnesota share are worse. They and their families have survived horrors that are among the worst that the modern world has seen.

There is a tremendous gap between Minnesota educators and the Somali immigrant students. This handbook is an attempt to fill that gap. Learning about another culture is a life-long undertaking. The first step in this rewarding journey is to contrast elements of one's own culture to the other. These baby-steps toward understanding another culture serve as the reference points that we so often refer to as "cultural differences." The differences that individuals choose to look at when first taking notice of another culture depend on their own culture and experiences.

It is important to point out that people of ethnic communities that are different from our own are often seen as having come from a completely monocultural environment. In fact, every society has various ethnic and cultural subgroups. Because of the nature of this handbook, we are forced to generalize, yet we caution against making assumptions based on stereotypes. For example, the cultural background needed to understand a student who comes from a rural, nomadic, extended family group would be dramatically different from the background needed to understand a student who comes from a middle-class Mogadishu neighborhood.

THE AUTHORS:
DON MCMAHAN'S STORY

I was born in Madison, Wisconsin, and in my neighborhood most of the kids came from Irish, Italian, or German Catholic families. I have only a vague understanding of what it was like for my grandparents and great-grandparents at the time that they came to this country. My mother used to tell a story that when her father's family immigrated, her grandfather's younger brother was separated from his family, lost in the throngs of people in New York City, never to be seen again. My father told a story about his parents planting wheat on a homestead in North Dakota, and the five years of drought that drove them to the city with nine kids in tow. My favorite was about my mother's long cold walks to school. Her mother gave her hot baked potatoes, wrapped in towels to put in her pockets to keep warm, and to eat for lunch. I know that my grandparents and their parents struggled to make a life here, and I know that my parents suffered through the Depression, but I'll never really know what any of that was like.

In fact, very few of us have even a vague understanding of what it is like for an immigrant or refugee to come to this country. Some time ago, a cab driver told me that his immigrant grandfather started out in a tarpaper shack on the outskirts of Saint Paul. Within a short time, and without any public assistance, the cab driver's grandfather had taught himself English, assimilated into the culture, and started working his way up the ladder. The cab driver explained that newcomers today don't deserve help. They should have to do the same as his grandfather did.

I know that my parents and grandparents had some very tough times, and that I have a tendency to romanticize the fragments of their experience that I know about, just like the cab driver did. I can even allow myself to imagine that they made sacrifices in their lives with my benefit in mind. I tried to explain to the cab driver that his grandparents lived in a very different world than contemporary immigrants do, and that in the first two to five years, his grandfather probably learned all of the English he would need in order to work as a laborer, and to provide or his family (Takaki, 1993). The skills and level of English that workers need today are much more specialized, and take many more years to learn. I told him that assimilation is an intergenerational process (Takaki, 1993), and that the immigrants of his grandparents' generation also formed insular communities and practiced their old-world ways, just as the more than 40,000 Somali refugees in the Minneapolis area tend to do today (Nelson, 2000).

Those of us who teach need to do what we can to understand who our students are and where they come from. When the Hmong began to settle in the Twin Cities in the early 1980s, there was very little information about them. Over time, books and papers were published, and experiences were shared. Today, the body of material about the Hmong people in their homelands and in America is substantial and still growing. Somalis have been coming to the Twin Cities area for a relatively short time, and the population is growing exponentially. Somalis who come to our schools are in a better position today than the Hmong were 20 years ago because today we have programs in place for English language learners. However, we have very few resources available for teachers to learn about who their Somali students are.

Somali refugee children present many challenges. In one of my classes, there were only four Somali students. By early October, three of them had already been suspended for fighting. In fact, by that time Somali students had been in conflicts all over the school. When a teacher asked our Somali bilingual parent liaison to phone parents about students' behavior, she said that she didn't have time to phone individual parents because there were so many fights. Instead, she planned to invite all the Somali parents to school at one time to talk to them about behavior expectations at school. This problem was endemic.

Somali children are having a very difficult time adjusting to school life. We have heard the hypotheses offered that perhaps the behavior problems stem from post-traumatic stress disorder following war and refugee experiences. We have also heard it explained that many of the men have been killed in war, and so women are taking on the role of family disciplinarian. The theory is that in a society where women are not encouraged to be assertive, they lack the authority in the family to discipline their children. The explanations are as varied as children themselves.

I'll never know what it was like for my great-grandparents to lose their child in a crowd in New York City, or what it was like for my parents to grow up during the Depression. Those of us who are not refugees ourselves can't know what it was like to leave homes and lives turned to rubble, and move far away to start again. We can however, share stories, learn from each other, and rebuild together.

Teaching is the act of sharing curiosity and passion. I've been sharing since 1991, after I completed a degree in Education at the University of Wisconsin. Curiosity about other cultures and places led me to accept a position teaching English at a Chinese High School in Taichung, Taiwan. That's where I met Leah Rempel, who is now my life partner *and* fifth grade teaching colleague.

We loved Taiwan, but among our passions was travel. We traveled to Korea, where we continued to explore and learn about other cultures. In Seoul we also wrote English teaching materials for an educational publishing company. Many of the titles that we wrote are still available in Korean bookstores.

After four and a half years abroad, we felt a little homesick, so we returned to the United States to settle down in Saint Paul, Minnesota. In this teaching position, I worked closely with Somali parents and educational assistants to help Somali students feel more successful at our school. I tried my best, but I didn't always feel like I knew what I was doing.

This was about the time that Leah and I had begun a master's program at Hamline University, and that we met a fellow student and Somali refugee, Mohamed Farid. If Somalia hadn't been consumed by civil war, Mohamed could have comfortably retired from an executive banking position. Instead, he found himself a world away, teaching and advocating for Somali families at an urban elementary school in Minneapolis. Mohamed articulately reflected the fears and the hopes of Somali parents. Mohamed talked and I listened, and wrote. This handbook is the product of my need to know, and Mohamed's need to advocate for his people.

Since Leah and I have completed our masters programs, we've moved again: this time to China where we both are teaching fifth grade at the American International School of Guangzhou. We're also awaiting the arrival of a new family member, a baby girl, whom we'll be adopting from a Chinese orphanage. I love our lives here, but I miss Saint Paul. I hope that this book finds its way into the hands of those educators who have a need to know about their Somali refugee students, and who are trying their best to help them adjust to life at school, but don't always feel like they know what they're doing.

TABLE OF CONTENTS

CHAPTER ONE

A Sketch of Islamic and Somali Culture

In this chapter, we summarize information that we believe provides essential background for understanding Islamic Somali culture: values, dispelling myths about Islam, language, religion, Islamic festivals and holidays, family roles, and the traditional Somali educational system.

Important Cultural Values

Somali culture is a blend of influences, including Islamic tradition, nomadic and urban cultures, and Western influences. Islam is also the common link Somalis share with Muslims all over the world.

Somali and Muslim values reflect the teachings and the applications of Islam. The basic human values of Islam include truth, honesty, charity, generosity, mercy, sympathy, trustworthiness, integrity, moderation, courtesy, discipline, and justice, abiding by promises and pledges, and accountability to Allah. Islamic teaching is so integrated into the fabric of Somali society that that it is often difficult to see where religious influences end and where local culture begins. The most highly valued deeds that Somali Muslims can perform are those that contribute positively to society, maintain harmony, and help preserve and perpetuate Islamic belief and practice.

Charity, for example, is a central tenant of the Muslim faith and highly valued by Somalis. A person who helps dig a well where there was no water or build a mosque where there was no place to gather for prayer, is a person who is living a full life. When a beggar comes to a Somali's door, he is not given table scraps and sent away. Instead, he is invited into the house for a meal, and he stays until he has finished eating. Somalis believe that charity helps to reserve a place in heaven (Dini, 2001).

According to the teachings of the Prophet Mohammed, "the path to heaven lies between your mother's feet" (Ahmed, 1969). As children grow up in Western cultures, they are taught to become independent of their mothers and fathers. In Somalia, whether you are five or 35, your mother will always be the nurturer and advice-giver. Children stay with their families until the day they are married, and mothers are mothers for life (Dini, 2001).

Mothers and children are highly valued. Childbearing begins shortly after marriage, and a woman's status rises as she has more children. Many Westerners have pointed out the practical implications of valuing a large family and motherhood in an agrarian society where there is a need for farm labor and geriatric care of parents and grandparents. After all, there are no pension programs or Social Security Administration in Somalia. The Prophet's words about the path to heaven, however, beautifully phrases the spiritual value that Somali people attribute to mothers and to motherhood (Dini, 2001).

Collective identity is important to Somalis. Somalis believe that a person who behaves properly and accomplishes many good things in his life is seen not only as a credit to himself and his immediate family, but also as a credit to his father and his forefathers (R.S.C., 1999). Showing respect is equally important. In Somalia, children do not refer to adults by name. Instead, they are referred to as "uncle" or "aunt." This reinforces respect for elders and the idea that all Somalis are part of a larger family (Dini, 2001).

Education is considered invaluable. The teaching of the Qur'an (Koran) is especially important because sharing knowledge of the holy book improves lives on earth and helps others to achieve heaven after death. Secular education is also highly regarded. Before the war in Somalia a relatively small number of people could attend school. Therefore, opportunity to become educated in the United States is not taken for granted.

In Minnesota, Somali parents usually want to become very involved in the education of their children. However, parental involvement is impeded by differences in language, culture, and the fact that many Somali parents do not know that they have a great deal to contribute. Therefore, Somali parents need to be invited to participate in specific and structured ways. There are some suggestions for involving parents throughout this handbook.

Somalis believe that a harmonious relationship with God, neighbors, and all of creation brings about good things. Disruption in that balance can bring about suffering. The reverence and respect for elders and women and the importance of religious faith and practice, run in stark contrast to the horrific events of the civil war. There is an unanswerable question that accompanies the understanding of these aspects of Somali culture: How could the atrocities of the Somali civil war have occurred? A Somali would frame the question in terms of collective responsibility: "What terrible thing have the Somali people done in the eyes of Allah to deserve this?" (Mohamed, 2001).

Dispelling Myths about Islam

Because of the violence in various parts of the Islamic world, many people in the West have developed prejudice against Islam and against Muslims. The Western press has incorrectly reported that the word *Jihad* means *holy war*, when in fact Jihad refers to the life-long struggle that a Muslim faces in trying to follow the ways of the Prophet Mohammed (Scott, 2001). Also, the word *Islam* means *peace* and Somalis, as Muslims, should offer peace wherever they are. Many non-Muslims wonder why, if Islam is a religion of peace, Somali Muslims are fighting each other and creating civil strife. Simply put, those who perpetrated the atrocities for the past 11 years in Somalia are in violation of the teachings of the faith. It is important to differentiate between true Muslims and those who only claim to be Muslims to perpetuate political or personal agendas.

Language

No discussion of the Somali language is complete without mention of the rich oral tradition of the Somali people. The values of the culture have been passed from one generation to the next through poetry, stories, and proverbs. Each speaker adds details and tailors the story to the audience. Each community has members who are considered to be sages by their ability to recite and create common experiences through spoken language.

In Western cultures that value the permanence, reliability, and reproducibility of the printed word, there is very little concept of the competencies that an oral tradition fosters. Older Somali people, who grew up never reading a single word, could listen to a story once and repeat it with exacting detail. These same elders could go to a court of law, listen to testimony, and recite it back to the court when the need presented itself. The memorization of the spoken word is a skill that is unneeded in a text-based, literate society, but taken for granted by those who live in a society immersed in the oral tradition.

The Somali language did not have a written form until 1972 (Putman & Noor, 1993). In that year the government decisively ended the debate about which writing system to apply to the Somali language. Those who advocated for the use of the Arabic script argued that Arabic script was easier to learn for those who were already literate in Arabic. They also pointed out that the Qur'an is written in Arabic and that the teaching of the Arabic script made access to the Qur'an easier, which would help people in their religious lives.

Those who advocated for the Roman script argued that the colonial languages of Italian, English, and French are written this way, and that the printing equipment, which was already in use by government, was equipped to produce Roman letters. In 1972, the secular argument won out when the government chose the Roman script and launched a nation-wide literacy campaign. Although the implementation of the campaign was haphazard, its lasting effect was the beginning of recorded history in the Somali language (U.S. Department of State, 1998). The benefits of the written word are immense, but they have come at the expense of the listening and memorization skills fostered in oral cultures.

Some Useful Phrases
Educators may find the following phrases useful when working with Somali students and families.
- *Assalamu Alaikum* (Peace be upon you) The spirit of this greeting expresses that you don't know what will happen to the other person during the time you are not together. Peace is stability and safety.
- *Nabad miyaa* (Are you in peace?)

Since the colonial period, Somalis have used the following expressions, which are translations from European languages.

- *Subah wanaagsan* (Good morning)
- *Galab wanaagsan* (Good afternoon)
- *Habeen wanaagsan* (Good night)

Religion

Somalis are among the more than billion Muslims in the world. There are an estimated 100,000 Muslims in Minnesota (Scott, 2001). Islam is a monotheistic religion. Muslims, however, do not believe in the divinity of Christ. Instead, Muslims believe that Moses, David, Jesus, and Mohammed were all prophets. Muslims believe that Mohammed was the last prophet who was born in 571 AD, and received the revelation of the Qu'ran at the age or 40, and died at the age of 63.

Somali Suni Muslims believe that there is one Creator, Sustainer, Cherisher, and Sovereign of this Universe, and that he governs the entire Universe. God (Allah) alone is the source and the fountain of all knowledge and, since the creator of life is one, life itself cannot be separated into temporal and spiritual sections. The role of man in this planet is to be the vice-gerent (khalifah) of Allah who follows his commands and strives to enforce them in the world. Among Allah's commands are the Six Articles of Faith and the Five Pillars of Islam. (Qur'an). Muslims cannot choose which parts of the belief and practice are convenient for them at a given time. Instead, Islam requires that the Articles of Faith and the Pillars of Islam are believed to be applied in their totality.
The Six Articles of Faith are stated in the Qur'an (Koran) as follows:
- believing that Allah (God) is one and has no partners (Baqara, verse 136)
- believing in the Angels (Baqara, verse 177)
- believing in Allah's books: Torah, Psalms, Gospel and Qur'an (Baqara, verse 136)
- believing in The Day of Judgment (Baqara, verse 177)
- believing in all prophets from Allah (Baqara, verse 136)
- believing that everything is in the hands of Allah (Baqara, verse 136)
The Five Pillars of Islam have also been a stabilizing influence on Muslim life for many centuries and have helped to limit the rate of change in all areas of Somali life.
- *Shahadah:* The profession of faith. To bear witness that there is no God but Allah and the Prophet Mohammed is his last messenger (Baqara, verse 136)

- *Sala:* Performing the five daily prayers (Baqara, verse 3)
- *Zakat:* Giving charity (Baqara, verse 136)
- *Sawm:* Fasting during the holy month of Ramadan (Baqara, verse 185)
- *Haj:* Making a pilgrimage once in your lifetime to Makkah for the Haji (Haji, verse 27)

Allah has given every human the ability to choose or not to choose his path but, according to Islam, if one chooses not to believe, that person will be accountable for his choice in the day of judgment. The accountability begins at the age of puberty for every Muslim. Parents are responsible before this time to teach their sons and daughters how to perform their responsibilities toward Allah and toward the creation around them.

Islamic Festivals and Holidays

The names of the 12 months in the Islamic calendar are Muharram, Safar, Rabi' al Awal, Rabi' al Tani, Jumada al Awal, Jumada al Tani, Rajab, Sha'ban, Ramadan, Shawal, Dhul qi'dah, and Dhul Haj. The months of Ramadan and Dhul Haj are especially important because these are the two most important festival times for all Muslims occur at the end of Ramadan and on the tenth day of Duhl Haj. The 12-month Islamic calendar follows the cycles of the moon. In order to avoid the confusion caused by the difference between the two calendars, Muslims all over the world follow the sayings of the prophet when the months of Ramadan and Dhul Haj will begin and end.

Ramadan is the ninth month on the lunar calendar. During this month, Mohammed received the first revelation of the Qur'an. Over a course of 23 years, Allah's messenger, Jibreal (Gabriel) came to Mohammed and taught him the Qur'an (Clarke, 2000).

The celebration of the Qur'an being revealed to Mohammed took place *Layl' at al-quadr*, or the Night of the Power (R.S.C.1999). On this holy night the blessings that Allah bestows for worshiping him are multiplied by 83 years and 3 months. For 24 hours, everyone stays awake to worship and to read the Qur'an. A great deal of charity is also given at this time.

During Ramadan, Muslims abstain from eating, drinking, and sex from dawn to dusk. During these times, Muslims must also protect their tongues, hands, eyes, and ears from use that would displease

Allah. The month of Ramadan requires self-discipline and brings multiplied blessings to Muslims around the world. It also teaches wealthy Muslims to be kind to the poor.

The day after Ramadan ends is called Id-al-Fitir (to break the fast). At this time, Muslims hope that Allah accepted their fasting. Also at this time, Muslims are required to pay special charity to the poor. Every person, young or old, in the Muslim household pays around five to eight dollars based on today's calculation. Parents are responsible to pay for the younger children and for their parents if the parents have no income. In order to get more rewards from Allah, people read and learn more about the Qur'an during Ramadan.

During the three-day Id-al-Fitir festival Muslim parents will excuse their children from school. Parents buy new clothes for their children and for themselves, and adults give gifts and treats to children and to the poor. Relatives visit each other, and Somali families prepare delicious and spicy food. Poor or unmarried relatives and friends are welcomed for the feast. Id-al-Fitir could be compared to American Thanksgiving in that Muslims celebrate their thankfulness that Allah allows them to eat and drink as usual during the rest of the year.

The last day of the Id-al-Fitir festival is a special time because Muslims from various ethnic backgrounds celebrate together and pray. Big prayer halls are prearranged long before the festival day. At prayer time, people greet each other and offer good wishes. They wear their best new clothes and go by all means of transportation to mosque early in the morning. The processions are colorful and beautiful. Many men wear Western-style suits, while others wear the Arabian-style *dishdashah*. The women wear dazzling colors embroidered with the gold and silver thread of Pakistani, Indonesian, African, and Chinese *hejab*.

The biggest Muslim festival comes two months and ten days after Id-al-Fitir. It is one of the Five Pillars of Islam and takes place on the tenth day of the twelfth month of the Muslim calendar called Dhul Haj. Haji symbolizes the courage of faith and Allah's mercy. According to the Qur'an, Allah asked his prophet Abraham to sacrifice his only son Ismail. Abraham agreed to do it, but, by the will of Allah, Abraham's knife ceased to slaughter Ismail. Allah spared Ismail's life, and angels brought a sheep from heaven for Abraham and his family to slaughter instead.

During Haj, Muslims slaughter animals and celebrate Abraham's success in Allah's test of faith. This celebration reminds Muslims to test the strength and courage of their own faith in Allah.

It is one of the Five Pillars of Islam to go to Mecca for the Haj once in a Muslim's life. Muslims who are unable for health or financial reasons are exempted. For those who make the pilgrimage to Mecca, the Haj is the greatest religious celebration of their lifetime. If Allah accepts their sacrifice, they return home purified and without sins. For this reason, as a person gets older, the urgency of making the pilgrimage increases. *Id-al-Aha* is the holiday at the end of the Haj.

Besides Id-al-Fitr and Haj, Somalis celebrate two national secular holidays. June 26 and July 1 are the two Independence Days when British Somaliland and Italian Somaliland became independent from their colonizers, and united to form the Somali Republic.

Family Gender Roles

In Islamic cultures, the family is built through marriage, and mothers and fathers have responsibilities that are very different, but equally important. Men are responsible for the sphere that exists outside the home, and women take care of the business of the household and the young children. Men provide food and shelter and take a greater role in guiding and disciplining children as they get older. Men also take on a greater role in the religious education of the children. When performed properly, traditional gender roles compliment each other, reinforcing Islamic values and social harmony. Although many Westerners may find this traditional Islamic arrangement outdated or unsatisfactory, it is important to remember that to Somalis who are not living among Westerners, a more "liberated" point of view is irrelevant.

Educational System

In traditional Somalia, people did not have to worry very much about their children. Youngsters could run wherever they pleased and be constantly under the watchful eye of aunts, uncles, and other relatives. They did not worry about their children at school, either. Parents could send their children to school and expect that all of their educational and spiritual needs would be taken care of by school faculty. It was expected that schoolteachers would be models of Islamic morality and teach by example. If problems did come up at school, teachers and principals were expected to take care of them (Yusuf, 2001). After school, if a child did not come home right away, parents would easily assume that he was with an aunt or an uncle who was feeding and taking good care of him (Dini, 2001).

Before being admitted to a Somali public school, young children needed to attend a Duksi, or a Qur'anic school. After that point, the public school system was modeled after schools belonging to the colonial powers. Students went to school six days a week, Saturday through Thursday for nine and a half months a year. They wore uniforms and sat neatly in rows, 40 to 60 to a classroom. The British and Italian systems stressed student discipline and rewarded a student's ability to absorb and reproduce information presented through text and lecture. Arabic and Qur'anic teaching methods are favored in Somalia, which also emphasize memorization and recitation.

There was never the infrastructure for education to become available to the majority of families. Therefore, if a student made a grave violation of the codes of behavior or did not make adequate progress, he could be expelled, making room for another. This rarely happened, however. In a system where all participants share culturally and religiously defined sets of expectations, and where those who fall short of those expectations are denied access, there are no discipline problems to speak of. Children who did not go to school in Somalia learned what they needed to know by watching adults and participating in daily activities. Young people continue to learn after they become adolescents, living with their parents or with their spouses' parents (Yusuf, 2001).

Most Somali students in Minnesota have no experience with the Somali system of education. They have either had their schooling interrupted or have never been to school at all. Most Somali parents remember how Somali schools were supposed to work, but the expectations were so different from those of American schools that Somali parents usually need help in understanding what teachers and administrators expect of their children.

CHAPTER TWO

A Brief History of Somalia

In this chapter, readers will learn about the tragedy of the civil war in Somalia. Of special importance is that the civil war was not a result of the inherent violence of Muslim cultures, but grew out of the imported influences of colonialism followed by communist military dictatorship, both of which contested Islamic beliefs.

In order to understand the reasons why so many Somalis were forced to leave their country, it is important to learn about the history of Somalia. Before the nineteenth century, Western historians had largely overlooked the region. This is due to the fact that the Somali language was only a spoken language until 1972. Somalis have always passed their oral history through poetry and stories from one generation to the next.

Pre-Colonial Period

Somalis enjoyed ancient trade and cultural ties with Egypt and the Arabian peninsula. Archeological finds and relics of the past demonstrate the connection of present-day Somalia to ancient Egyptians, who traded in the region and brought home the precious scents of frankincense and myrrh. Among the best references of the early history of Somalia is a book by Richard Burton, called *First Footsteps in East Africa* (Waterfield, 1966).

The strong connections that the Somali people have enjoyed with the Arabian peninsula were strengthened by a common religion. Somalia embraced Islam as early as the time of the Prophet Mohammed 1400 years ago. At that time, some of his companions migrated to the region that is now called Ethiopia. Islam continues to shape Somali culture and maintains Somalia's connection to the rest of the Islamic world (U.S. Department of State, 1998).

Colonial Period

In the nineteenth century, Somalia was part of the Ottoman Empire, and then, in 1884, was divided by European colonists into five parts (U.S. Department of State, 1998). From the Somali perspective, the colonial division of the area was more than an historic event. It was the first domino to fall in the chain of events that led to the civil war almost 100 years later.

A book titled *The Somali Peninsula* (Information Services of the Somali Government, 1962) described how the colonists divided the Somali-speaking population into several geographic areas. The British held a region called the Northern Frontier District (NFD). In 1962 the British gave NFD to Kenya. The British-controlled Haud, Reserved Area, and Ogden, were given to Ethiopia. Somali people decried the separation. They believed that a people who believe the same religion, speak the same language, and share the same ethnicity should also share a nation (The Government of the Somali Republic, 1962).

Independence and Cold War

In 1960, British Somaliland and Italian Somaliland became independent states and united to form the present Somali Republic. One of the goals of the new independent state of Somalia was to unite the entire Somali territory under one flag. The strategies that the new Somali Republic used to achieve that goal created tension between Somalia and the neighbor states of Ethiopia, Kenya, and Djibouti. These tensions forced the new government to take sides in the international arena at a time when the Horn of Africa region was becoming a hot spot for the Cold War (U.S. Department of State, 1998).

The Cold War was a time when the United States and the Soviet Union were enticing weaker nations to ally themselves with either NATO or WARSO powers, training armies and equipping them with the machinery of modern warfare. The Soviets and the Americans were intensely interested in the area because of the Horn of Africa's strategic location, south of the oil-rich Middle East.

The Soviets endorsed the Somali cause, while the United States of America strengthened its friendly ties with Ethiopia and Kenya. The

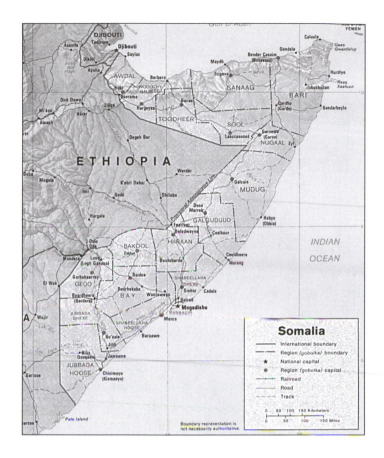

American government trained and supplied heavy weapons to the Ethiopian army and the Soviets trained the Somali army and sold heavy armaments to Somalia. This unbalanced regional situation led the Somali government to spend most of the country's available resources building a strong army, leaving less and less for roads, schools, hospitals, and other essentials. In spite of this, building the army received great support during this time because of the nationalist ideal of bringing all Somali people under one flag (Putman & Noor, 1993).

Military Dictatorship

By 1969, Somalia had enjoyed only nine years of civilian government. It was in that year that the Somali President Dr. Abdirashid A. Shermarke was assassinated and Major General Mohammed Siyad Barre took power. Barre allied himself more closely with the Soviet

Union, which brought the communist system to Somalia. The Soviet model banned the free market economy, challenged the Islamic way of life, and continued the social and cultural disintegration that eventually led to civil war. Privately owned business was banned; industries, private companies, and banks were nationalized; and the government centralized the economy under the Soviet model (R.S.C., 1999). When Barre took over power in Somalia, international trade was confined only to the communist world and the business community lost status and influence.

The Islamic social order began to fray. Younger generations received forced communist party political orientations and massive military training. They grew up without learning Islamic law or traditional family values. Wise and knowledgeable community leaders were arrested and replaced by ignorant and unpopular government-appointed personalities (U.S. Department of State, 1998).

With the support and advice of the Soviet KGB, Siyad Barre went about eradicating his opposition. He targeted families, friends, and clan members of the ousted civilian regime, and executed or arrested many intellectuals, religious scholars, and politicians as enemies of the state. From the beginning of his rule, Barre used his alliance with his own clan to build the core leadership of the military and the secret police. This manipulation of one clan against another intensified hatred among clans, making the resolution of normal conflict between them increasingly difficult. This clan hatred is the fuel that would later ignite at the onset of the Somali civil war (R.S.C., 1999).

In 1974, the Ethiopian monarch, Halie Selassie, was overthrown. Somali rebels within Ethiopia revitalized efforts to liberate Somali-speaking areas in that country for annexation into Somalia. American and NATO influence was curtailed in Ethiopia and a Marxist military dictator took power. In 1977, a war erupted between Somalia and Ethiopia and Siyad Barre ousted the Soviets from Somalia and changed his allegiance to the United States. The Soviets responded by intensifying their support for the Ethiopian military government. The Soviet experiment was over for Somalia, but the Somali people were living with the aftermath of militarization and Soviet-style economic nationalization (R.S.C., 1999).

Post-Communist Somalia

People did not understand how to live with the centralized economy where the government was the only provider. The age-old religious and cultural traditions of charity, family, and community cooperation that Somalis had practiced for so many centuries were damaged, along with free enterprise and market competition. The vacuum created by the political, social, and economic changes imposed upon Somalis in the years before 1977 could not be filled by any alternative that Barre's military regime attempted to provide.

As people began to feel the poverty, those with education and means began to leave Somalia to look for opportunity and freedom in the nearby Arab countries, which were enjoying an unprecedented economic boom fueled by petrol dollars. The flight of educated workers aided the downward spiral of the Somali economy (R.S.C., 1999).

The Slide into Anarchy

In this way, a combination of colonialism, followed by military dictatorship and communist philosophy, prepared the way for poverty, hatred, injustice, corruption, nepotism, and spiritual emptiness in the social, economic, and political circles of Somali life. Also, most Somalis are of nomadic background and move from place to place according to the needs of their camels, sheep, goats, and cows. Their livestock is the only property they respect, so they do not have strong allegiance to land or political boundaries. Nomadic Somali people freely crossed between Somalia, Kenya, and Ethiopia and hated the colonists for creating these artificial lines that impacted their lives and restricted their movements (Putman & Noor, 1993). Over the years, the various Somali government administrations, comprised of urban-dwelling people, offered little or nothing in response to the grievances of this majority sector of the population. They believed that the nomads lagged behind in Islamic and secular education, which they saw as basis to understanding and respecting civil life and civil obedience.

Under Siyad Barre's military dictatorship, traditional leaders who had knowledge and wisdom were jailed or removed from their posts, and factional clan conflicts were manipulated. Nomadic peoples were armed and given military training. The use of the nomadic peoples to serve the interests of the government and warlords caused great destruction and led to one of the worst human atrocities of modern times (U.S. Department of State, 1998).

By the mid 1980s, the government militias and opposition movements were clan-based, and Somalia slipped into anarchy. A tragic irony of the Somali civil war is that food and medicine provided by the United Nations was one of the most powerful weapons that perpetuated the violence. By the mid 1980s there were no agencies left inside the borders of Somalia to deliver humanitarian aid. Shortly after the food and medicine arrived inside Somali borders, it fell into the hands of clan leaders, and was used as payment to militia members who were becoming increasingly desperate in their struggles to provide for themselves and their own families. Those who were not allied with a powerful enough group became victims of violence and starvation (Ali, 1998).

From Ravages of War to the Diaspora

Before the civil war broke out in full force, Somalis were leaving. The privileged and the educated people left first. With their connections, resources, and language skills, they were able to escape the worst of the bloodshed. Later, many of their immediate families and extended family members were able to find their way to safety through sponsorship. Many of those who experienced the worst of the war and the refugee camps were the less educated and less fortunate. Rich or poor, educated or uneducated, any Somalis who could not find safety tried to ally themselves with clan forces or became targets of bandits (Ali, 1998). Women and children suffered most.

At the beginning of the civil war, women were spared. Militia from one clan searched homes belonging to members of rival clans with the intention of executing the men. At this stage in the war, women were protecting their husbands and sons by hiding them in any way that they could, often by dressing them in women's clothing and attempting to transport them by cover of night to areas where no fighting was taking place.

As the war went on, women became targets as it became apparent that they were actively protecting their men. In an attempt to create fear among the women and dissolve their support for their male family members, women were gang-raped and often killed while the children stood by helplessly. There were even instances where women who took refuge with their children inside mosques were raped and killed there. The clan militia often carried the dead bodies of raped and murdered women to well-visited public places as a warning to any woman who would dare protect her brother or husband. Infants were collected by the militia and left outside hospitals with signs inviting passersby to take the helpless infants home (Ali, 1998).

Women and children fled by any means available. If they had a car and gas to run it, they took all of their portable valuables and drove in search of safety. The car was often confiscated by clan militia and people inside were questioned, looted, raped, and either killed or left to die on the roadside. Starvation, dehydration, and disease showed no mercy on the survivors.

The roads from Mogadishu to the interior of Somalia were littered with the bodies of the murdered and infirm. Those who could, just kept walking. By 1992, more than 1.5 million people were in danger of starvation because of the civil war and 45 percent of the population had either escaped the country or were displaced from their homes (Putman & Noor, 1993). The only hope for the people who survived the 500-mile trek to the border was that the Kenyan government would take pity on them and let them cross to safety (Ali, 1998).

The Kenyan government had recently been at war with Somalia and did not see any advantage to getting involved in the Somali civil war. Kenyan officials also took very little pity on the starving, humiliated hordes amassing at their border. It took considerable pressure from the United Nations to finally open the Kenyan border to Somali refugees. United Nations provided humanitarian aid under an agreement with the Kenyan government that the Kenyan government administer that aid. By May 1993, the UN had taken over the command from the United States. Operation Restore Hope had been partially successful in stabilizing the situation, but the Somali government and infrastructure of the country had been destroyed (Putman & Noor, 1993).

Ramshackle refugee camps were quickly set up, and chain-link fences were built around them. Pilfering of food and medicine by officials was commonplace, and mismanagement and corruption led to more malnutrition, starvation, and disease. To make matters worse, the lack of proper policing in the camp compounds led to more rape and robbery. In most cases, those who were responsible for policing and maintaining the refugee camps were the perpetrators. Children were often deprived of food until a relative who had already escaped could sponsor them. The application process through the United Nations for a host country took a very long time. Children who were left orphaned in the camps became low priority, and many languished there for as long as five years (Dini, 2001).

Many of the children who are now in United States schools grew up in refugee camps. During that time their parents had plenty of time to imagine what their lives in their new homes might be like. In order to build hope, they offered their children stories about how wonderful their new lives would be once they were given permission immigrate to a host country. In silence, they wondered if their children would survive to see it.

Post-war Trauma

We retell this history of the war and refugee experience of the Somali people because it is important to learn why Somalis have come to the United States. We also need to be aware that an estimated 35 percent of Somali refugees have been tortured, and all of them have experienced the loss of everything (Williams, 2001).

Every Somali has been deeply affected by the civil war. Many live with the guilt, anger, and fear that stems from that history. The suffering continues in Minnesota. Somali people in Minnesota share grocery stores, mosques, and neighborhood streets with members of other clan groups whom they suspect were responsible for their suffering. Somalis, however, are reluctant to discuss the sensitive issue of differences between the various clans and ethnic groups because of the overriding desire to live together in peace.

Children who may have been too young to remember the war in their homeland feel the effects of the civil war. Their parents, aunts, and uncles tell the stories of their narrow escapes over and over, as lessons to the children that they should take advantage of the new opportunities that their parents' struggle has opened up for them (Yusuf, 2001). Meanwhile, the fear and distrust, infused by more than a decade of torture and instability, has become a mode of existence for many, and is passed on to the next generation (Center for Victims of Torture, 2000).

Why Minnesota?

Most Minnesotans do not know much about Somalia, but they might well imagine that it is about as different from Minnesota as two places on earth can be. It does not make sense to the average Minnesotan that so many Somalis would have chosen to come from arid, equatorial East Africa to the freezing, northern upper-Midwest. To refugees in the camps and to other Somalis who were desperately looking for missing relatives or waiting for bureaucracies to finish paperwork, differences in climate were not important. The promise of being reunited in peace and prosperity was the only thing that mattered.

Somali history and culture, steeped in the oral tradition as we have noted, has been accelerated by the telephone, the postal system, and the Internet—perhaps a good reason why so many Somalis chose to settle in Minnesota. One refugee told another that Minnesota had plenty of jobs, good schools, and excellent refugee services. The word has spread very quickly among a population desperate for new beginnings.

Those beginnings were not without problems. In the early 1990s there was already a growing number of Somali refugees in Minnesota. Many of these pioneers had noticed that new incoming Somali refugees of various clans and ethnic groups were bringing with them the animosity and hatred that had destroyed Somalia. Somali people were not even greeting each other on the street. Somalis understandably carried the suspicion that any other Somali who was affiliated with a different clan or ethnic group could have been involved in the decimation of their families and lives (Center for Victims of Torture, 2000).

At that time, a group of Somali-American community leaders invited representatives of 17 different clan and ethnic groups to meet and to recognize their need to come together and to help each other. That event was a dramatic success. The message of reconciliation spread from that meeting of 17 elders to the entire Twin Cities Somali community. From person to person, family to family, the word continued to spread around the globe to Somalia and the refugee camps of Kenya and Ethiopia and back to the American cities where other Somalis refugees had already settled. That message was that Minnesota is a good, peaceful place to live. The message of a good life and of reconciliation spread as a banner of hope.

As time went on, Somalis began choosing Minnesota for more practical reasons: family and community. Somali people have always relied on the support of large extended families for survival. People continue to move here because they know that they will be supported and guided by family.

CHAPTER THREE

The Stress on Somali Families in Minnesota

In this chapter, information focuses on societal and economic situations and issues that bring stress to Somali families who live in Minnesota. Everything that affects families also affects children and their ability and willingness to learn at school. This is why it is important to look beyond the walls of the school to understand how to help students become ready and willing learners

Housing

The transition from Somalia to Minnesota has not been easy. Most Somali people have chosen to live in specific Minneapolis neighborhoods because of low housing prices and the availability of public transportation. People continue to move to these neighborhoods because of the concentration of services provided in the Somali language. Also, since Muslims can only eat meat slaughtered according to Islamic law, *halal* (lawful) grocery shops and restaurants are important. Mostly, Somalis move to these neighborhoods for social activity, availability of religious services, and for the social support of the larger Somali community.

However, since Somali families traditionally live in large, extended-family groups, one- and two-bedroom urban apartments are inadequate for their needs. The availability of affordable apartments large enough for their family groups is very limited. Family members who themselves have been in the country for a very short period of time have become "experts," helping others to find housing (Husen, 2001).

The lack of adequate affordable housing has forced many people to move several times in the course of a year, sometimes falling victim to unscrupulous landlords who take advantage of an applicant's lack of English skills or knowledge of American rental procedures (Nelson, 2000). In the search of low rent, many Somali families find themselves in neighborhoods where they do not feel safe. Gunshots heard at night remind them of the war and their escape, so they may not allow their children to go outside. Somali people who might earn enough money to qualify to buy a house may choose not to because of Islam's prohibition on borrowing money in exchange for interest. In this way, many Somali families are frustrated by the search for affordable housing with little hope of someday buying a home.

Some Somalis have moved to Saint Paul because of marginally cheaper rents. The first tier of suburbs around the Twin Cities is also seeing an influx of Somali families for the first time. Some Somalis are even moving to smaller outlying communities for affordable housing and because they feel that the rural environment makes it easier to maintain their Islamic traditions (Reabe, 2001). This secondary migration out of Minneapolis to other areas is presenting a host of new challenges for Somali families and for schools.

Isolation

Outside of the Minneapolis neighborhoods where Somali people are concentrated, the language barrier becomes a much more pronounced problem because people are less insulated from the English-speaking dominant culture, and also because interpretation and translation services are not as readily available. There are also complaints that they are unable to find suitable *halal* (lawful) food in the supermarket, and that transportation is more difficult. In Minneapolis, there are many Somali-run businesses and a simple request to a relative or a friend would be enough to get a ride to the doctor's or dentist's office. The new suburban or rural environment can be especially difficult for women who carry tremendous responsibilities taking care of their families with less support from friends and relatives. Also for the women, the isolation in a setting where they have fewer social contacts can become emotionally overwhelming (Dini, 2001).

Finances

"Did you get your 3:00 a.m. phone call?" Before coming to the United States, many Somali refugees heard stories that exaggerated the positive side of life here. The day they arrive, many would almost believe that "they can scoop money out of the Mississippi River," so the high cost of living is unexpected for most new arrivals (Yusuf, 2001). New arrivals learn quickly that there is never enough to cover the bills. To compound the problem, most refugee families are under constant pressure to send money to relatives in Somalia. The communal society in Somalia has survived for thousands of years in part because of the emphasis on helping family and giving charity. When the telephone rings at 3:00 a.m., and a relative asks for help, it is impossible to say no (Yusuf, 2001).

Taking Care of Relatives

"If you have only twelve in your house, you can take fifteen!" (Yusuf, 2001). Among Somalis there is an expectation that family members will take care of each other. So, once a family finds an apartment and gets settled in, distant family members often arrive, expecting to move in with them. When that relative goes away, another comes to take his place. This revolving door puts pressure on families who are already living in spaces that are too small for their needs. These families are under additional pressure to keep their guests secret, because leases usually restrict the number of people who are allowed to live in a rented unit. The revolving door can also put children in a difficult position at school. When teachers or classmates ask Somali students who lives with them, kids are forced to lie or give ambiguous answers. They may fear that if someone in authority finds out, their family could be forced out of their home (Yusuf, 2001). In the meantime, housing prices continue to rise at unprecedented rates, pressuring low-income families to look elsewhere for cheaper places to live. Wherever the housing is available, people are moving.

Taking Care of Children

The pressure of raising children properly causes a great deal of stress in every parent's life. For Somali parents in Minnesota, the responsibility for raising children is complicated by the fact that their children are learning two languages and two cultures simultaneously.

In Somalia, parents were never expected to participate at school, even regarding discipline issues. But when kids came home with homework, parents could usually help. In Minnesota, parents are called in to deal with misbehaving children, and Somali parents feel pressure to help their children with homework that they do not understand. One Somali man from a rural part of Somalia was quoted as saying, "In Somalia, I took care of animals. In the U.S., I take care of kids!" (Husen, 2001). The statement was not meant to be a demeaning comparison of children to animals, but rather an illustration the difficulty that Somali people are raising their children in a culture of which they are not a part.

Most seriously, as Somali children learn the English language and American culture, they tend to drift away from Islamic and Somali values. This drift is seen as more than just a threat to maintaining Somali cultural pride and identity. Islamic law must be followed in order to reach heaven, and it is parents' responsibility to raise their children to follow that law. The consequence of failure is an afterlife in hellfire.

Role Reversals

Another stressor for Somalis is the reversal in family roles. We mentioned earlier that in Islamic cultures, men are responsible for the welfare of the family in the public sphere, and women have domain over the private sphere of family life. However, so many men were killed in the civil war, and many of those who have come to Minnesota have found that the skills that earned a living for their families in Somalia are irrelevant here. As a result, many of those men have become depressed and unavailable to help their families (Dini, 2001). This puts tremendous pressure on women to earn a living for the family and to fend for themselves in the public sphere.

As children get older, another role reversal takes place. Children become proficient in English before their parents do. They also more quickly adapt to the host culture. As a result, they are called upon to act as interpreters for their parents, and to represent their parents to the English-speaking public. Boys especially, in absence of adult males, feel the pressure to take on the responsibility of the head of family before they are ready. Another aspect of this role reversal is that it often puts children in authority over their parents. Especially for adolescents, the temptation to circumvent parental authority is irresistible (Husen, 2001).

Individual Responsibility

Compounding the pressures on Somali refugees in Minnesota is the seemingly insurmountable pressure of individual responsibility. The Somali identity is tied in with the framework of a large, extended family, so it is inconceivable to Somalis that anyone would have to do anything absolutely alone. Separated from family members, and immersed in the dominant culture that emphasizes individual accomplishment, Somalis can be left feeling powerless (Dini, 2001).

Depression

There is no word for "depression" in Somali. Pressures on Somali refugees in Minnesota, combined with memories of wartime atrocities and loss, makes many Somalis tired of the effort it takes to live in the United States. Deskilled fathers, and mothers who have lost other children to war may not believe that they are adequate parents to their children who have survived (Dini, 2001). One high school girl became weary of her mother's constant weeping. In her search for a way to help her mother, she went to the library and "discovered" that there was something called depression (Yusuf, 2001).

Accommodating Somali Students in Public Schools

This chapter is intended as a resource for teachers and administrators who are looking for ways to accommodate Somali students' religious and cultural practices in public schools. The topics in this section were selected to provide answers to questions about Islamic practices and how the cultural tensions and misunderstandings they can cause may be overcome at school.

Each topic is introduced by a brief vignette, using fictional teachers and fictional students. The situations represented in the vignettes, however, come from the collected experiences of the authors and some of the authors' colleagues. Following each vignette is an "explanation." This portion contains some background for understanding the cultural conflict represented in the vignette, as well as some insights and suggestions for teachers who may be experiencing a similar situation.

Vignette 1: Getting Oriented

It was 9:15 on the first day of high school. Ali was looking for room 303. Moments before the hallways were bustling with activity, but now Ali was alone in the hallway. He wandered up and down the corridor on the first floor, comparing a number written on the piece of paper that he held in his hand, to the room numbers embossed on the classroom doors. In fact, Ali had grown up in a rural part of Somalia where he had never been in a building that was more than one story high. He had not yet learned that he would find room 303 by going up the stairs to the third floor.

Explanation. Many children who come from rural Somalia have very little experience with urban life. If available, bilingual support can smooth the transition immediately after arrival at school. The same children who have difficulty searching for a room in a multi-story building might also have never used a combination lock or a calculator. The proper way to use a sink and a toilet may also be fairly new. Children who are very young may learn about these aspects of urban life with minimal embarrassment, but older students may be deeply embarrassed by their lack of experience with these matters.

Also, while the weather is still mild in the autumn, most of us do not think about the impending winter very much. Somali families who have recently arrived and who have never experienced a winter in the upper Midwest need to be made aware of the type of clothing that they and their children will need when the weather gets cold. They also need to be told about the proper footwear needed to avoid falling on the ice.

Another suggestion for recent arrivals is to be aware that most of them have come with a very high level of expectation of how wonderful school will be and how beautiful life in America will be for them. The hopeful images that they hold in their minds quickly lose luster when compared to the reality that they experience. When they arrive, instead of finding themselves in wealth and comfort, some have found themselves in homeless shelters where they are greeted by the elements of our society that we ourselves try to ignore. This experience of disappointment can create hostility (Nelson, 2000). If a teacher can provide an outlet for that disappointment through journaling or some other means, the students will make a happier and more comfortable transition to life in the United States.

Vignette 2: A Simple Handshake

It is the first day of school, and everyone is excited about the new school year, even Mr. Carlson. Mr. Carlson has been the principal for seven years, and his favorite part of the job at the beginning of the year is greeting students and parents as they come into the building on the first day of school. He especially enjoys reassuring the parents of first graders who nervously guide their children to the school, hoping to catch a glimpse of what it will be like for their kids. Mr. Carlson is

*a middle-aged Minnesotan who prides himself on never forget-
ting a name, and being able to put parents and children
immediately at ease.*

*Mr. Carlson had heard that the school was going to be get-
ting a new first-grade student from Somalia. He had
thoughtfully made some preparations. He had checked with
the cafeteria to be sure that there would be alternatives to
pork on the menu, and he had spoken to the ESL teachers in
the building, asking them for advice.*

*He knew that the Somali people had suffered greatly in a
civil war. Beyond that, he didn't know what to expect. He
had the highest level of confidence in his staff, and knew that
they would do their best for this new student. All he could
do was to do his best to make this parent and her son feel as
welcomed as possible in school.*

*He saw Mrs. Nur approach the school with her son
Mohamed. She wore the traditional dress, the hajeb, which
covered her completely, except her hands and her face. She
smiled nervously. He approached to greet her, automatically
extending his right hand, reaching with his left to touch her
elbow. He had welcomed thousands of parents over the years
with this very same handshake.*

*Mrs. Nur's clenched her fist and jerked away. Her nervous
smile had turned to an expression of shock. For a long, awk-
ward moment, Mr. Carlson and Mrs. Nur just stood looking
at each other. What had gone wrong?*

Explanation. What Mr. Carlson was not aware of is that Islamic law
does not allow physical contact between men and women who are not
in the circle of those you cannot marry (like a mother, sister, daughter,
etc.). When he reached out his hand to shake Mrs. Nur's hand, she
became uncomfortable not because he had done something insulting or
embarrassing, but because this is a gesture of greeting and friendship
that she could not reciprocate. A friendly smile and an affirming nod
will be enough the next time Mr. Carlson greets Mrs. Nur.

Vignette 3: Names

Aasha was a troubled girl, and Mr. Cornel felt that he needed to know more about Aasha's background so that he could help her. Mr. Cornel started by looking up Aasha's school record. He wanted to know how long Aasha had been in the country and if she had any brothers or sisters in at school.

Recorded at the top of the girls' cumulative file was her full name, Aasha Ali Mohamed. The file also reflected the fact that Aasha had a brother in the sixth grade. His name was Khalid Ali Mohamed. Listed as her parent or guardian, however, was Faduma Omar Abdullah.

Mr. Cornel thought that he had found part of the answer. "That poor girl," Mr. Cornel thought. "Aasha must be an orphan. Faduma Omar Abdullah must be a relative who is taking care of the children in the United States. Both of her parents must be dead. No wonder she's such a troubled girl!"

Explanation. Mr. Cornel assumed that since the person listed on the form as guardian did not share a last name with Aasha and her brother, that Faduma Omar Abdullah was not their mother. In fact, it is normal for women not to change their names when they get married.

The way that children are named illustrates an interesting aspect of Somali culture. Generally speaking, every child is given a first name at birth. This name is usually followed by the father's name. The third name is the name of the child's grandfather. So, in fact, Aasha Ali Mohamed means "Aasha, daughter of Ali, granddaughter of Mohamed." Since Aasha's lineage cannot change, neither can her name after she eventually gets married.

By extension, if you assume that the patrilineal chain of names could go on for a very long time, you are right. There are those who can recite names from their father's through their great, great, great, great, great, great grandfather's, and beyond. This naming system gives Somalis the sense that they are all part of one large extended family and reinforces the sense of familial relationships and responsibility among Somalis.

It is also important to note that some confusion is often experienced in the documentation regarding the names and ages of children enrolling in school in Minnesota. Many of the families came from the nomadic life where written records are not known. Urban Somalis may share this problem because birth certificates were destroyed or lost in the war.

Vignette 4: Pork

Faduma was a new student in the school. Ms. Rodriguez, her teacher, was keeping a close watch on Faduma. She wanted to be sure that Faduma was making a good transition to life in an American school. She made a special effort to greet Faduma as she got off of the bus in the morning, and she went out of her way to encourage Faduma in any way that she could. For the first four weeks of school, however, it never occurred to her to check on how Faduma was doing at lunch.

One day she went to pick up her class after lunch and one of the lunchroom supervisors said, "You know, I have never seen that girl eat anything. Do you suppose she's anorexic?"

There was not a bilingual aid at Ms. Rodriguez' school, and Faduma could not explain for herself why she was not eating anything at school. Finally, when an interpreter arrived, they discovered that Faduma thought that all of the meals on the lunch menu contained pork. All of the dishes served were radically unfamiliar to her, and she was unable to distinguish between the different kinds of meat.

Explanation. A hot dog seems pretty innocuous to most of us, but there is almost no difference in taste or appearance between an all-beef or turkey hotdog and one made out of pork. To someone who does not know the English language well enough to ask, a chicken patty sandwich and a plate of lasagna both contain mystery meat. "Hot dog" may even be understood literally as "hot *dog* meat."

According to Islamic law, pork is not allowed. Neither is anything made from blood or from animals not slaughtered by Muslims, Jews, or Christians. In Somalia, people do not need to think very much about dietary restrictions because non-halal (non-lawful) meat is simply not served.

Newcomers from Islamic countries may suspect that most unfamiliar American foods contain pork, and may refuse to eat anywhere but at home. Also, the typical school lunch contains nothing that looks or smells familiar to Somali newcomers. If Somali children are not reassured that the food served in the school cafeteria is completely free of pork, they may refuse to eat.

Teachers need to advocate for Muslim families for pork-free food in the cafeteria, so that menu planners do not serve it. If pork is served in any form, Muslim students should be specifically made aware of it. Teachers can also help students and their families by teaching students how to identify pork products listed on food labels.

Vignette 5: Prayer

When the school started to get a few Somali students, providing a place to pray was never a problem. Mr. Beal simply put up an office divider in his classroom to provide a small space and enough privacy for prayer. As the Somali population started to grow, however, so did the problem of finding prayer space. The problem became unmanageable during the month of Ramadan. First of all, during the holy month, more students than usual expressed a desire to pray. Secondly, the population of Somali students at the school had doubled since the previous year. Space was at a premium in the school. Mr. Beal was going to have to find a larger space for Somali students to pray.

Explanation. Prayer is the devout Muslim's daily reporting to Allah and is one of the most important pillars of Islam. When a Muslim goes to prayer, he is talking to Allah. He recites passages from the Qur'an and bows his head repeatedly to the floor. Upon finishing the prayer, he comes back to this world. On the day of judgment, a Muslim's first accountability will be his prayer. One of the greatest concerns that Somali Muslim parents have is that their children will not get the religious education they need in a secular school. One of the simplest things we can do for those parents and their children is to provide a space for children to perform their midday prayers.

All practicing Muslims are required to pray by the age of puberty, called "the age of responsibility." After the age of responsibility, all

Muslims are responsible in front of Allah, so they must perform all of the requirements in terms of belief and performance. Training for prayer begins at the age of seven, so many children are required to pray at school before puberty.

The performance of each prayer should take between five and ten minutes. The schedule is published by the local mosque and is dependent on the Islamic lunar calendar. All that is required is a clean place that is private enough so that the students do not attract undue attention. An unused classroom or the library is usually fine as long as there is clean space on the floor. Students will need to visit the bathroom before prayer in order to perform ablutions, which is a ritual washing of their hands, face, arms, legs, and head.

Friday prayer is a special time. Unlike other prayer times, Muslims do not close themselves off to the world and speak only to Allah during Friday prayer. Instead, Muslims come together to pray and to discuss the ways in which they can account for themselves and improve their Islamic practice. The Friday prayer is led by an Emam. Any member of the congregation can serve as the Emam, but he is usually the most knowledgeable in the teaching of the Qur'an.

In some high schools, parents are allowed to come to school and take their children out for Friday prayer. In one Minneapolis school, the principal made an arrangement with a neighborhood church for students to congregate at a scheduled time on Fridays. Since students can lead the prayer themselves, teachers and administrators do not need to involve themselves with the religious purpose of the meetings.

Vignette 6: Fasting

Ms. McGowan thought she was ready for the Holy Month of Ramadan. She collected materials about the holy month and taught all of the students in her class about it. Her Muslim students were enthusiastic about sharing their experiences. When the Ramadan began, however, she realized that the school was not ready for the particular problems that fasting created for her Muslim students.

Lunchtime on the first day of Ramadan started routinely. The kids lined up at the door and she led them down the hall to the cafeteria. As the rest of the kids lined up to get their lunches, the Muslim kids went straight to the tables and sat down. They sat hungrily in their seats and watched the other kids eat.

Explanation: Ramadan is the ninth month on the lunar calendar. During this month, Mohammed received the first revelation of the Qur'an. Over a span of 23 years, Allah's messenger, Jibreal (Gabrial) came to Mohammed and taught him the Qur'an. Since that time, Muslims celebrate Allah's gift of the Qur'an by abstaining from eating, drinking, and sex from the morning prayer to the evening prayer for the entire month of Ramadan (Clarke, 2000).

Unlike the Gregorian calendar, based on the pattern of the earth's rotation around the sun, the Islamic calendar follows the pattern of the moon. The first day of Ramadan changes a little bit every year so that every 33 years it returns to the same date on the Gregorian calendar.

During Ramadan, Muslim students will be hungry, and they may not want to go to the cafeteria and be tempted by the food. It is particularly uncomfortable for them to have to sit next to other students who are eating, while they cannot partake of a glass of water to drink. Teachers and administrators who are sensitive to their students' needs will find an alternative to the cafeteria for these students during lunchtime.

It is important to realize that not all Muslim students fast during Ramadan. After the age of seven, parents encourage children to fast for the purpose of training, but it is not absolutely required for children under the age of puberty. So, children under the age of responsibility may choose to fast one day, and then choose to eat lunch the next.

There are some who are exempted from the fast during Ramadan. Pregnant women or mothers who are nursing can choose to postpone their fast to a time later in the year. People who are recovering from illness may do the same.

One of the biggest problems that schools have in trying to accommodate students who are fasting during Ramadan is finding a place and supervision during that time. Many schools in Minneapolis and Saint Paul allow students to go to the media center or library during their lunchtime. Of course, proper supervision is essential, and teachers and administrators or parents need to provide that supervision. Ideally, parents should be invited to come to school to supervise during Ramadan.

If students are behaving improperly in the library, teachers should feel free to send students back to the cafeteria to sit at a separate table where the other kids are not eating. Fasting may be one of the Five Pillars of Islam, but being free of temptation is not. Having an alternative to the cafeteria during Ramadan is a privilege, not a right.

Vignette 7: Physical Education

Mr. Hanson is the physical education teacher. He believes that in order to be fair, all students should be treated equally. At the beginning of the year, the principal came to Mr. Hanson's office to tell him that several Somali Muslim kids had enrolled in the school and that he would have to find ways to accommodate them. The principal told him that, among other things, the Somali girls would refuse to participate in athletics with the boys, and that they also would not dress in gym uniforms.

Mr. Hanson became upset that he had to go so far out of his way to accommodate Muslim students. Every year he had kids who refused to participate in swimming or basketball because it made them uncomfortable. His policy was not to allow anyone to sit out without a note from a doctor for a medical exemption.

Explanation: The problem that many Muslim parents and children have with physical education classes in American schools is not that Muslims object to athletics or that they are required to expose their bodies, violating Muslim dress codes. The problem is that these classes are usually co-educational. Girls are welcome to participate in sports, but not in the presence of boys. When they are in the presence of boys, girls must have their heads covered, and there must be no physical contact. A simple game of tag between boys and girls is prohibited according to Islamic tradition. In a coed physical education class where there is only one Muslim girl, she should be allowed to sit on the sideline with a friend and watch. If there are several, the school could provide an alternative class or possibly tutoring sessions.

There are also Islamic dress codes restricting the dress of boys and men. According to the Islamic dress code, boys and men must be covered from above the navel to below the knee, and they are only allowed to be naked in the privacy of home. Gym uniforms, swimming trunks, and showers may be problematic. When Somali boys go to a public shower, for example, they may bring a towel with them to cover themselves. Religion aside, they are culturally unaccustomed to being in a locker room where students undress in front of each other. Physical education teachers should be sensitive to Somali boys' modesty and consider providing privacy for those boys who ask for it.

In the case of girls and boys, it is important to keep in mind that there are varying levels of practicing Islamic rules of behavior. Many Somali girls are perfectly comfortable participating with boys in physical education classes without their parents' knowledge. Somali boys may not think twice about dressing for a swimming class and taking a shower with their classmates afterward. Their level of participation depends on their level of acculturation to American culture and their level of practice in Muslim tradition. Another thing that physical education teachers should be aware of is that during the holy month of Ramadan, their Muslim students will probably not be allowed to eat or drink anything during the day. Under these conditions, strenuous activity could lead to fatigue and dehydration.

Vignette 8: Music Class

Mr. Jones is the music teacher at the school. When he heard that there would be some Somali students coming to the school, he was excited. He felt strongly that music was the international language, and he was enthusiastic about teaching kids from diverse backgrounds. In his experience, students with limited English skills were successful in his class, whereas they often struggled in others. When Mr. Jones received word that the new Somali students would not be taking his music class, he was stunned and disappointed. He went to the principal to find out why.

Explanation: Western music, from classical to pop, expresses everything from Christian spirituality to sexual love. Devout Muslims believe that music in the Western world inappropriately brings females and males together. According to Islamic law, that is not allowed. Therefore, many parents prefer that boys and girls not participate in music classes.

However, this is a choice that parents make. When there is no alternative, Somali students are forced to go to music class. Without an alternative to music class, some parents become frustrated with the school and may look for another.

If there are only a few Muslim students who prefer not to participate in music, they could go to the library, or receive additional ESL or bilingual instruction at this time. In a school where there is a large Somali population, parents could be invited to the school on a rotating basis to teach the children anything they like, thus strengthening the connection between home and school.

Vignette 9: Using a Song in a Lesson

Mr. Jefferson loves to use music in his ESL lessons. He uses recordings of popular songs from past decades to give his history and social studies lessons context. He has also found creative ways to use songs to teach vocabulary, grammar, and the rhythm of language. He feels that music is also highly motivational for most students, and that when he connects his lessons to music, kids remember what he taught.

This year, however, Mr. Jefferson has stopped using music altogether because one of his Somali girls has objected every time Mr. Jefferson has taken a CD out of its box. "We can't listen because of our religion," the girls reminded him. Without the music Mr. Jefferson feels that his lessons are missing something. He could not make the connections for his students that he once could. He also resents the fact that something that can be so helpful and is so innocent as a song should be prohibited.

Explanation: There are Somali families who so strictly adhere to Islamic rules about music that they would disallow it altogether in the classroom. The concern is that music is so often used in a social environment where boys and girls come together, encouraging them to become sexually active. It would not be acceptable, for example, to play the radio in the classroom during a period of free time. If an individual student chooses not to participate when music is played during a lesson, he or she should be allowed to leave the room and do something else during that time. If parents complain, it may also be necessary to communicate to them about the value of the music in the lesson, and the context in which music is used in the classroom.

Vignette 10: Art Class

Mr. Moon teaches art at the school. When he first found out that there would be some Somali students assigned to his class, he decided to do a little research on the artwork of Somalia. He learned that the artistic traditions of Somalia range from the arts and crafts of the various nomadic peoples who range in the desert of the Horn of Africa to the fine artistic traditions of the Islamic world, which incorporate beautiful intricate geometric designs with an overriding sense of balance and symmetry. Mr. Moon liked to decorate his classroom with examples of the artistic traditions from his students' cultures.

Mr. Moon also knew that all kids loved cartoons. His first assignment of the year was for students to copy drawings of Mickey and Minnie Mouse. As his students were starting to work, he noticed that two of the Somali kids were scribbling and breaking pencils. The third was drawing a beautiful flower.

The entire period, he struggled to get the three Somali students on task. The Somali students were frustrated too. They told Mr. Moon that they could not draw. In the end, Mr. Moon sent the scribbler and the pencil breaker to the principal's office as punishment for being noncompliant.

Explanation: When the scribbler and the pencil-breaker told Mr. Moon that they could not draw, they may have meant to say that they were not allowed to draw the image of a person or an animal. During the time that the Revelation was sent to the Prophet Mohammed, there were 360 different idols being worshipped. Allah revealed to Mohammed that the worship of idols was a great sin. As a result, Islam has banned the reproduction of the human image and the images of animals.

In fact, Muslims are taught that, on the day of judgment, Allah will put any image that they have made of people or animals in front of them, and challenge them to breathe a spirit into the drawing. Creating the image of a living thing is considered by Allah to be the ultimate in human arrogance. Thus, in Muslim homes, you are unlikely to find images of people or animals. If Mr. Moon had observed Islamic art and architecture more carefully, would have realized that they were also free of such images.

In short, the most devout Muslim students should have no problem participating in art classes, as long as they are not required to create human or animal images. Mr. Moon simply needs to provide alternative assignments for Muslim students.

Vignette 11: Health Class

Ms. Baber has been teaching health at the high school and the middle school levels for seven years. Part of the curriculum is to teach students about responsible sexual behavior. Ms. Baber does not yet know if the new Somali students in the school will be participating in her class. If they are enrolled, she wonders, how will she be able to teach the required curriculum?

Explanation: Most Muslim parents believe that the discussion of sex with children is solely the responsibility of parents. According to Islamic beliefs, there is an appropriate time for fathers to speak to their sons, and for mothers to speak to their daughters about sex. School districts have provisions for parents who do not want their children to participate in sex education classes. It is extremely important that parents are informed about the content of health education classes, and be given the opportunity to exempt their children from participating in the discussion of sex in those classes.

Vignette 12: Dating

Just before Valentine's Day, Ms. Levine thought it would be nice to teach a unit on dating and courtship around the world. She had collected some high-interest reading materials on the subject, and she hoped to use them to help her students compare and contrast dating rituals around the world with those of the United States. She also thought that comparisons like these might help students to explore the dating rituals of their own cultures.

The day that Ms. Levine introduced the lesson she sensed that her Muslim students were uneasy with it. She was not sure exactly what their objections might be, so she decided to talk to a bilingual staff member about it. After that conversation, Ms. Levine cancelled the unit.

Explanation: A topic like dating challenges Islamic tradition. In Islamic cultures, the structure of the family is to be in accordance with Islamic law and is built only through marriage. The process of marriage is a collective responsibility of the couple's families and the arrangements start long before the marriage contract is established.

In the West, choosing a wife or a husband is usually a matter of the heart, and is an arrangement between individuals. In Islamic cultures, choosing a wife or a husband is not only to satisfy a person's emotions but also to choose the right mother or father for future children. This collective responsibility of both families and individuals makes the marriage decision wiser and, therefore, divorce is less common. Also, to have children who are born outside marriage is against the Islamic teaching and is a crime committed against the law of Allah.

Dating is allowed in Islamic cultures, but takes place in a different fashion than the Western world. According to the Islamic law, Muslim girls are allowed to marry only Muslim men and only after obtaining the permission of their parents. Men, on the other hand, are allowed to marry Muslims, Christians, or Jews.

A date consists of a meeting between the two families so that the bride and groom see each other only in the presence of their mothers, fathers, or other relatives. Men and women who are eligible to marry each other are only permitted to meet privately after the marriage contract is established. In this way, parents and the couples work together to build the family in a carefully calculated and responsible manner. Financial support and counseling are provided to the new family from both sides.

Vignette 13: Clothes

In Ms. Genin's second-grade class, there are three Somali girls and three Somali boys. At the beginning of the year all of the Somali girls came to school wearing jeans and T-shirts much like the rest of the students. The Somali girls fit right in with the rest of the students. One day, however, Amal came to school wearing the traditional hejab *that Ms. Genin had seen Somali women and older girls wear. The other students in the class also became curious about Amal's change in dress. In fact, Ms. Genin had to break up a fight over it. A non-Somali student told Amal she covered her head because she was so ugly. Naturally, Ms. Genin also became curious and began to quiz Amal about her new outfit. Ms. Genin was surprised when Amal was reluctant to tell her why she was the first Somali girl in the second grade to wear the* hejab.

Explanation: Somali girls are in a difficult position. At home they want to be traditional, and at school they want to be like all of the other kids. Islamic law requires that women be covered from head to toe, except for their face and hands whenever they are in public. Jeans, for example, expose a woman's shape, so they are not allowed. Somali girls are encouraged to wear the *hejab* after the age of seven for the purpose of training. At the time of their first period or after the age of 15, they are required to wear the *hejab* by Islamic law.

Puberty is referred to as "the age of responsibility." Before that age, parents are responsible for the spiritual guidance and religious education of the children. After 15, the children themselves are responsible in the eyes of Allah. The social pressure to wear the *hejab* is considerable. If a girl chooses not to wear the *hejab*, she might be thought of as less than a decent, proper lady, and she is told that that she may have difficulty finding a proper suitor. At home, wearing the *hejab* for the first time is a rite of passage for Somali girls, but in American schools it can become the flashpoint for ridicule.

Between home and school, Amal is stuck. There are several things that Ms. Genin might have done to have made Amal's first day wearing her *hejab* easier. First, she might have prepared her class for the Somali girl's inevitable change of dress by giving her Somali students the opportunity to share with the class why Somali women dress the way they do. Bestowing public compliments on Amal, telling her that she looks beautiful in her new *hejab*, would have bolstered Amal's confidence and sent the signal to the other students that her new outfit was something special, not to be ridiculed. Also, inviting a Somali adult into her class to discuss Somali culture and dress might have helped non-Somali students to understand their classmates. Adolescents especially need validation to feel strong and confident in themselves at time when their bodies are rapidly changing. The sharing of cultures in the classroom also helps validate Somali culture for all students.

Vignette 14: Halloween

All kids love Halloween. That's what Mr. Duffey thought. Every October he decorated his room with black cats, ghosts, and witches. He even used to have a costume day where everyone dressed in ghost or goblin outfits, until a small, vocal minority of Christian parents complained to the school board that the school's participation in pagan rituals was an affront to their religious beliefs.

spite of the prohibition, Mr. Duffey thought that since he was now teaching ESL to kids from other countries, that it was his job to teach them about American holidays and customs. He decorated his room in orange and black jack-o-lanterns, ghosts, witches, and black cats, only to discover later that now his Muslim students' parents were complaining.

Explanation: Halloween can put Somali children squarely in the middle between what their parents expect and what is accepted at school. When Somali kids come home and excitedly tell their parents about the strange celebration in which they participated, their parents may forbid it and tell them that it is contrary to Islam. Given the opportunity, all kids want to eat candy and dress in funny costumes. Muslim kids who participate, however, may fear disobeying Allah and their parents.

Vignette 15: Homework

Abukar does not do his homework. Ms. Dupris has contacted his mother and explained through an interpreter that is important for Abukar to spend at least an hour every night completing his lessons. She has agreed to check with Abukar every evening and to help him in any way that she can.

Although Abukar's mother cannot read and understands only rudimentary English, she sits down with her son every evening and asks him to read his work to her. This arrangement worked for about a month, but after that time Abukar's work starts to slip again.

At parent-teacher conferences, Ms. Dupris expresses her disappointment over Abukar's progress. Abukar's mother tells Ms. Dupris how she checks her son's homework on a nightly basis. As it turns out, Abukar has been taking advantage of his mother's lack of English and knowledge of school subjects. Instead of reading his homework to his mother, he has been selecting random pieces of his past work to read to his mother at night (Yusuf, 2001).

Explanation: It is especially difficult for refugee parents, who speak little or no English and who are unfamiliar with the American school system, to help their children with homework. Although there are no easy solutions to this problem, several things have been tried. One middle school established a "homework hotline" where teachers provide a daily list of homework assignments to interpreters who made an announcement on a recorded telephone message. Parents may call the homework hotline number and listen to a list of homework assignments in their own language.

Teachers can also design homework assignments that encourage parental participation. One teacher created a unit where students went home and asked adults about Somali folktales. Students made picture books about the folktales that their parents told them, and then read the folktales in English to their parents during the parent-teacher conferences. Another solution is for tutors to come into the home and help children with their homework. In Minnesota, tax credits are available for low-income parents to pay for tutoring services (Thompson, 2001).

Another problem involving homework is that there is often a lack of quiet time and space at home for students to complete their work. Teachers can help by encouraging parents to schedule quiet time for homework. Most importantly, teachers should be sensitive to this problem and vigilantly seek out ways to involve parents in their children's academic work.

Vignette 16: Race

For the most part, Shara was adjusting very well to life at school. She was learning English quickly and keeping up with her homework. Her life was often made miserable by a group of American girls who ridiculed her for the way she spoke and for wearing her hejab. One day, as Shara was waiting for the bus, two of these girls demanded that Shara give them her money. Shara was terrified. Since she did not have any money to give them, the girls pushed Shara, called her names, and threw her backpack into a muddy puddle.

Shara did not want to tell the principal at school because she was afraid that if the girls knew that she had told, she would be attacked again. After her experience with this group of girls, Shara has also been very careful to avoid contact with other Americans she encounters.

Explanation: It is sad that Shara is developing a prejudice against Americans based on her experiences with a group of bullying girls, but this is why teachers need to be especially sensitive to their Somali students' developing awareness of race and racial stereotypes, and be open to discussing them.

In a school with a large Somali, Hispanic, and American population, for example, one group of Somali students was overheard using "nigger" to refer to some of their African American classmates. After some discussion with their teacher about the impact of racial epithets, it became clear that the Somali students had innocently heard their Hispanic classmates using the appropriate Spanish term, "negro," and assumed that both terms were the same.

By comparison to the United States, Somalia is a homogeneous country. In fact many Somali students who have recently arrived in Minnesota may have never seen a white face except for pictures in a magazine or in a movie. The concept of a diverse multicultural community, with all of the complexities of differing culture and race, is inconceivable. In America, the concept of race is much more complex than a shade of brown or tan. Privilege and discrimination, lack of opportunity and affirmative action, are all affected by how we are perceived by others according to race. For these kids the complexities of race in America is incomprehensible.

For a Somali student in a predominantly white school, racial tension is also an issue. When that student is introduced to a racially charged environment, he or she may be the last one in the room to understand the motivation behind discrimination.

Vignette 17: Gestures

Ali loved loud, physical play. He liked to wrestle with his friends and to make a lot of noise while doing it. This always got him into some trouble at school, where that kind of play was not allowed indoors.

When Ali initiated a wrestling match with a friend in Ms. Armstrong's class, Ms. Armstrong shouted Ali's name to get his attention. When Ali looked her way, Ms. Armstrong gestured for Ali to "come." She held out her clenched hand and repeatedly curled her index finger toward herself. Ali became angry. He shouted something back to Ms. Armstrong in Somali, and then reluctantly came over to where she was standing.

Explanation: Without knowing it, Ms. Smith insulted Ali. In Somali culture, "come" gesture is respectfully performed with the palm open, the hand sweeping toward the speaker. Gesturing for someone to come with the index finger pointed upward, is reserved for dogs.

There are a few other gestures that have specific meaning to Somalis.

- Holding both index fingers parallel to each other means "same."
- With an open hand, a quick turn of the wrist means "nothing" or "no."
- Finger snapping means "a long time ago" or "so on and so on."
- Pointing your shoe or the sole of your foot at another person is very impolite.
- The "thumbs up!" gesture is considered obscene to Somalis.
- Winking at a member of the opposite sex is offensive.

CHAPTER FIVE

Effects of Refugee Experience on Somali Children

Most refugee children who come to our school system adjust very quickly and remarkably well, considering gaps in education and hardships they have experienced. Unfortunately, many Somali children have not adapted well. From our own experiences and through our conversations with other teachers who work with Somali students, inappropriate behavior is an overriding concern. For example, students engage in fights and teachers complain that Somali boys do not show respect for female authority figures.

In Chapter 2, we included a few graphic details of atrocities experienced by some Somali refugees. In this chapter, we attempt to explain where some of this aggressive behavior may come from by making a connection between war and refugee experiences, and misbehavior in school.

Somali Adults' Explanations

The misbehavior that we see exhibited by Somali students in school was unheard of in Somalia before the war. Somali parents expect their children to respect and obey their teachers completely. When teachers report that their children are not showing that respect, they are deeply dismayed and embarrassed.

Some Somali adults perceive persistent misbehavior as stemming from two sources. The first source is that the misbehavior is learned by example from American kids. In Somalia it is unheard of for a student to refuse to follow directions or talk back to a teacher, but in urban American schools, defiant behavior is common. Somali refugees who have relocated to Muslim countries have encountered much less trouble with misbehavior at school. It is only natural to assume that some of the negative behavior in American schools is learned by example from American students.

The second source of misbehavior is perceived as being the destruction of the family and the erosion of Islamic values through the war and refugee experience. The result is behavior exhibited by children that Somali adults do not consider normal. School staff and non-Somali students may see these behaviors and falsely attribute them to Somali or Islamic culture. In order to make the distinction clear, we have chosen to define persistent misbehavior as being part of a "refugee culture."

What is the refugee culture? Most of the Somali children who have come to Minnesota have not had the benefit of a stable family life by any description. For example, Somali kids who are currently in high school were young children in the chaos of civil war. They grew up in refugee camps, where starvation and day-to-day survival set the rules of behavior. The significant adults in their lives were also struggling to survive, and to protect whatever shreds of dignity they had left. The children spent their days almost unsupervised, without even the benefit of basic schooling. Refugee communities were shattered by war, and so were the traditional values of Somali and Islamic culture. Many Somalis view the children who grew up in this environment as difficult to fathom because they do not behave like Somalis.

There is a common perception among Somali adults that the weakening of the family structure has resulted in a lack of proper Islamic training and discipline on the part of the young generation. The circumstances that led to the horrible civil war in Somalia had been on the horizon for a very long time before the war began. The communist government's campaigns to undermine the religious traditions of Somalis planted the seeds of decay in the traditional Somali way of family life. The military dictatorship and the corruption and disorganization of the new communist political system were major contributors to the civil war that ultimately destroyed the Somali social and family fabric and its Islamic way of raising children.

The civil war did more than just upset the delicate balance of the traditional Somali family. During the war, the men did what they could to protect their families. Many took up arms to either defend their families or to join in the fighting, hoping that the faction that they supported in the conflict had a chance of winning. Many thousands were senselessly killed in full view of their wives and children. Some of the lucky ones left the country with the intention of preparing a place for their families to join them later. Some families were eventually reunited; most were not. Other men stayed behind in Somalia, sending their families away hoping that they would find safety.

Single mothers were unheard of before the civil war. In a world where their men are dead or missing, single mothers are courageously forging ahead into unprecedented territory. In the Somali experience, there are no role models of strong single women holding down a job and taking care of children, but this is what they are doing here in Minnesota. Fathers, who have always been responsible for the education and discipline of older children, are often absent.

Many women who have never lived in an urban environment before and have always had the support of a large extended family are facing some unexpected challenges in the Twin Cities. They often work two jobs, live in a small apartment, and raise not only their own children but also the children of relatives who are missing. For those who are raising children of relatives, their job is especially difficult because they and the children may not even know if the parents are alive or dead. This may bring about feelings of abandonment, resentment, or worse. Many of these kinds of problems are dealt with on the community level, and may not be visible in school. In spite of these challenges, Somali women are very concerned about the education of their children and eager to be invited to participate in the life of the school.

Many Somali women are unprepared to teach Islamic values to a high standard because they generally have received less training in this area than Somali men have. There have simply been more opportunities for men to pursue religious education in Somalia. This is a concern because Islamic values hold Muslim cultures together. To Somali people, the lack of order in society is directly attributed to the erosion of those values. This lack of order ranges from the brutality of civil war to a child's misbehavior in school. The restoration of Islam in the minds and hearts of Somali young people is viewed as essential to the success of children and to the survival of a healthy Somali community in Minnesota.

In the words of Mohamed Farid, coauthor of this handbook, the misbehavior of Somali children in American schools is persuasively explained:

> *"If children are traditionally brought up, carrying the values of Islam with them, there is no problem. If they lose that, then we don't know about them. We can't explain. If a person goes away from the values and traditions, then they go away.*
>
> *The civil war has caused people all over to become more faithful, because this is what saved them. Many young teenagers in the refugee camps survived using drugs and doing Islamically unlawful things because they were faithful believers and feared Allah and the hellfire after death. Many learned the Qur'an in the refugee camps and demonstrated great success in school and employment when they came to Minnesota.*
>
> *I remember a young lady who was in my school who did not know the ABC's but she knew the Qur'an. When I started with her she was so smart. By the time she came to high school, she was only in the country for three years and she passed all of the Basic Standards tests."*

The effect on the children who lived through the war and refugee experience without the fortitude of faith has been sometimes tragic. The "refugee culture" has become the norm of many of their lives. Children who were raised in refugee camps have spent formative years without schooling or adequate adult care. Even if parents have the time for their kids, they are not mentally present to teach the kids right from wrong and proper family values. Children play in the camps as years go by while their parents or relatives are busy thinking of ways to get out of the refugee camps. Refugee children learn street language and develop behaviors strange to their culture and parents. The fear is that these children of the refugee culture may be a lost generation.

Vignettes Related to Classroom Management and Discipline

In this section, we present a nine more vignettes. Once again, the names of the students and teachers are fictitious, as are the details of each situation. With this set of vignettes, we focus on aspects of misbehavior at school. In doing so, we recognize that there are no easy answers, but we try to offer some suggestions.

Vignette 1: "They're tearing the building down!"

Ms. Olsen was the assistant principal in charge of discipline, and the school year was off to a rocky start. By mid-October discipline referrals and suspensions all over the building were disproportionately high among Somali students. They were fighting on the bus before school, in the halls, and in the classrooms. For each fight, she called the students who were involved into her office, along with the bilingual staff member to discuss what happened. Parents were called, and some kids were suspended. There were so many fights that Ms. Olsen and the bilingual support person were exhausted. Everyone was thinking the same thing, "There's got to be a better way!"

Explanation: This scenario played itself out at the school where one of us works. A bilingual staff member called all of the Somali parents to the school for a meeting, and encouraged them to bring food to share. Many of the parents had already been called to school to talk to the staff about the behavior of their children, and they were just as frustrated as the teachers and administrators were.

At the meeting the principal and staff explained to the parents exactly what the problems were, what the discipline policies at school were. Effective coordination between school and parents was very helpful in reducing misbehavior at the school.

It also helped that as the school year went on, we teachers got to know the students better, and we were better equipped to help students avoid or resolve conflicts before they developed into physical fights. Classroom community circles, where students had opportunities to communicate in constructive and positive ways, also contributed to a more positive environment for students. Teachers helped individual students who had difficulty controlling their anger, reminded students of the consequences of fighting, and then offered alternatives like a cool-down period in a quiet place. The most effective deterrent to fighting in school, however, was the Somali parents. Their involvement dramatically improved the school climate.

Vignette 2: Post-Traumatic Stress Disorder

It was the fourth week of school, and Ms. Rouser was generally happy about the way the school year was unfolding. When her students came into the classroom in the morning they were usually happy and ready to learn. Every day, however, she struggled with Abdullah.

When Abdullah came in, he sat by the window and looked outside. When it was time to begin, Ms. Rouser turned the lights off and on as a signal that it was time to begin. The rest of the students went to their seats and prepared for reading time. Abdullah continued, staring out the window.

Ms. Rouser walked over to Abdullah and gently put her hand on his shoulder and asked him to move to his seat. Abdullah exploded in a fit of anger and shouted loudly at Ms. Rouser in Somali. Ms. Rouser did her best to console him, but instead she had to step back from him to avoid being hit by his flailing arms. The rest of her students took advantage of the distraction to get out of their seats and move freely around the room. Ms. Rouser called for a bilingual interpreter to help her communicate to Abdullah how important it was for him to follow directions and to go to his seat so that he and the rest of the class could carry on with the lesson. Abdullah was inconsolable. The interpreter told Ms. Rouser that Abdullah believed that Ms. Rouser hated him and that was why she was forcing him to do something that he did not want to do. Ms. Rouser knew that Abdullah needed help, but she had no idea where to turn.

Explanation: In the history section of this handbook we briefly described the atrocities that many of our students witnessed during the civil war, the survival skills that they have developed out of the harsh chaos and uncertainty of the refugee camps, and the stress of learning a new language and surviving in a foreign culture. If we could learn more specifics of Abdullah's past we might be able to conclude that he is suffering from post-traumatic stress disorder (PTSD). The *Guide to Working with Young People Who Are Refugees* (1996) describes PTSD as anxiety that is caused by "…having been exposed to life-threatening situations or intolerable danger, where the victim has been helpless to act (Victorian Foundation for Survivors of Torture Inc. p. 1.3.1)." The *Guide* goes on to describe the kind of behavior that is often seen in students who are survivors of war. "With the pressure of anxiety and tension which the young person cannot manage, he or she may become highly irritable, be unable to tolerate frustration of any kind and thereby show reduced control over impulsive behaviour and aggressive behaviour" (*Ibid.*, p. 1.3.1).

The following is quoted directly from the *Guide* (p. 1.3.1):

Summary of Affects Associated with Anxiety
- Intrusive and recurrent distressing recollections of the traumatic event
- Impaired in ability or think, concentrate, and remember
- Conditioned fear response to reminders, places, things, and people's behavior, leading to:
- the avoidance of fearful situations
- the restriction of imaginative play
- emotional withdrawal

Generalized fear not directly related to trauma:
- The fear of strangers
- The fear of being alone
- The fear of dark places
- Hypervigilance or watchfulness:
- "Being on guard for danger"
- Startle responses: reacting with startle to sudden changes in environment such as noise
- Capacity to manage tension and frustration is reduced
- Emotional numbing
- Re-enactments of traumatic events in play
- Psychosomatic complaints, e.g. headaches
- Regressive behavior, e.g. tantrums

Impulsive and aggressive behavior often means fighting. Before students who are suffering from PTSD get into in a fight, they may find themselves suddenly experiencing the fight or flight response and lose control of themselves. Tracey Psycher, a teacher in an area high school, has compiled a list of suggestions for de-escalating fights involving a survivor of PTSD. The following list is adapted from her pamphlet entitled *"Classroom Management Strategies that Work"* (Psycher, 2001).

- Use a clear, forceful voice. Shout: "Stop! Now!"
- Never approach a fighting student from the front. Approach from the side to redirect attention away from the person with whom s/he's fighting.
- Humor can be used to redirect attention.
- Use eye contact with the student to dissolve the tension.
- Mediation is often very useful. Often survivors of PTSD overreact to perceived threats. Once they have regained composure, they may be open to mediation.
- Talk to students individually about classroom behavior. Do not confront them in front of their peers.

Above all, Psycher reminds teachers not to engage in power struggles. Survivors of post-traumatic stress disorder will not back down if they are feeling threatened. It is much more effective to stay calm, keep your sense of humor, and avoid imposing threats (Psycher, 2001).

Mirjana Bijelic, the Minnesota schools project coordinator for the Center for Victims of Torture has compiled a list of classroom interventions to help teachers in their work with survivors of post traumatic stress disorder (Bijelic, 1998). The following list is quoted from her pamphlet entitled, *"Working Effectively with Schools to Address the Needs of Refugee Children"* (Bijelic, 1998).

- Address the experience of being different.
- Use creative productions (art, essays, etc.) as vehicles for expression, understanding and healing.
- Provide structure, consistency, safety, nurturance.
- Prepare students for change; facilitate transitions.
- Address trauma as a potential factor in learning and behavior problems.
- Normalize trauma reactions.
- Recognize and honor students' strengths as survivors.
- Provide opportunities for refugee students to teach others about themselves and their experiences.
- Provide opportunities to do important tasks for their family and community (especially important for adolescents).
- Link students with school "buddies" or mentors who can provide support and learning about how the school works.

More Vignettes Related to Classroom Management and Discipline

We present seven additional vignettes, which we hope will provide some context for a few of the issues raised by Psycher and Bijelic. The first of the vignettes, however, is an attempt to explain how many people in the Somali community may be resistant to the discussion of mental heath issues.

Vignette 3: "Allah will provide for us."

> *Mohammed is the most challenging sixth grader Ms. Hawn ever had. He had been suspended for fighting several times. He constantly challenged his teachers' authority and demanded their attention. One very difficult day, Ms. Hawn started her lesson with the following announcement, "Please open your books to page 29." All of the books were opened, except Mohammed's. As Ms. Hawn began reading to the class, Mohammed began to chant, "What page? What page!" Another student told Mohammed which page to turn to, but he ignored her and chanted more loudly "What page?...WHAT PAGE??" Rather than addressing Mohammed's inappropriate demand for attention directly, Ms. Hawn addressed Mohammed's need to know the page number by saying, "If you look at the bottom of page 29, you will see...."*

> *Mohammed was often moody, unpredictable, and sometimes violent. Ms. Hawn believed that something was deeply wrong with Mohammed. She knew about the bloody Somali civil war and the conditions in the refugee camps. She wondered if Mohammed might be experiencing some kind of post-traumatic stress disorder. She talked to the school counselor, and he agreed that it was possible, but there would be no way to tell without some psychological tests.*

> *Ms. Hawn and the counselor asked Mohammed's mother to come in to meet with them. A bilingual staff member joined them and they all met in the counselor's office. Ms. Hawn explained to Mohammed's mother about her son's behavior at school. Mohamed's mother was distraught and apologetic, but not surprised. The counselor asked Mohammed's mother*

a few general questions about Mohammed's background before coming to the U.S. and then recommended that they seek psychological testing for her son.

Mohammed's mother was not receptive to the idea of psychological testing at all. To Ms. Hawn and the school counselor, she seemed to be a very defensive about the issue. Through the interpreter she told them "Allah will provide for us."

Explanation: People who experience major traumas in their lives may have difficulty trusting others, nightmares and flashbacks, and impulsive aggressive behavior. A Western psychological explanation might be PTSD. Most Somalis do not see the world through the same lens as Westerners do. The reasons a Somali Muslim might give for aberrant behavior are not psychological at all. They are spiritual, and so is the cure.

Every culture has its own way of healing. The Prophet Mohammed said, "Indeed amazing are the affairs of a believer! They are all for his benefit; if he granted ease of living, he is thankful. And if he is afflicted with hardships, he perseveres; and this is best for him" (Qur'an). In Somali culture and according to Islam, people believe that it is almost impossible to have a stable life in this world. This is against the nature and Allah's natural laws. Thus, life on earth is full of surprises and trials that come in small cracks or heavy crashes. This varied nature of life is what makes life livable and enjoyable.

Can you imagine life that is always happy or always sad? Happiness or sadness would become meaningless. Alternating times of happiness and dismay, strength and weakness, wealth and poverty, health and sickness, make life tough and make life enjoyable. Such changes have another purpose.

A true believer of Islam is one who maintains a clear level of Emaan (believing and practicing the Six Articles of Faith and the Five Pillars of Islam) throughout the trials and tests of life. A true believer continues to remember Allah and ascribe the bounties to him when times are good, and turns to him in submission when asking for relief for his affliction when harsh times come. If one succeeds in that, life becomes good, regardless of whether he is happy or sad at any given moment.

The struggle to survive the Somali civil war and its trauma are facts of life. It is a continuous process for Somalis in Minnesota and across the globe since the problem has not been solved or settled so far. It has also affected the children and their behavior drastically. Children were malnourished in the refugee camps and did not have the opportunity to enjoy adequate parental care or education. This refugee experience taught the Somalis that the more a person believes and practices Islam, the better he survives the trauma. The problem we are facing is that the kids are lacking Islamic education and are therefore developing the behaviors of saying bad words, fighting, and lying. However, the parents of these children and the adults who are true believers of Islam survived because of Emaan (their belief in Allah) and their hope that Allah will give them relief very soon.

Mohammed's mother's objection to psychological testing may also have a cultural basis. In the Somali language, a person is either crazy or is not crazy (Williams, 2001). She may have thought that the teacher and the counselor were insulting her child with an accusation that he was crazy. It is extremely important for interpreters to be trained to sensitively explain these important issues to parents.

Vignette 4: "I don't have to listen to you!"

Ms. Curtin had dealt with a lot of stubborn boys in her teaching career, but Awaale was the most stubborn she had ever met. If she asked the class for their attention, Awaale was always the last to be quiet. When she asked the class to take out their notebooks, Awaale would sometimes do it, other times he would flatly refuse. One day Ms. Curtin took Awaale into the hall to remind him that she was his teacher and that she deserved more respect than he was giving to her. Awaale was not apologetic. He told her that he did not have to listen to her because she was a woman.

Explanation: If Somali boys display such behaviors toward female teachers, it does not mean that they particularly disrespect them. It may be that some boys use their cultural background as an excuse for their poor behavior, or that they are ignorant of the good behaviors, both Somali and American.

It will take some students time either to correct this in the positive Somali way or the American way. For the American female teacher, learning the cultural background about genders in the Islamic culture is an important aspect of working with Somali students so that the miscommunication will be avoided and suitable student-teacher relationships will be developed. The Somali boys in Minnesota, according to their culture, should respect their female teachers as their mothers, and take their orders and make sure that teachers are pleased with them. But according to the refugee culture or adopted American culture, the behavior of the boys is strange to the Somali mothers, sisters, and the other female relatives.

At ages from birth to four, Somali children have closer ties to their mothers than their fathers. Mothers are the most effective parents for younger children. Young children tell their secrets to their mothers. When children are young, the role of the father is mostly to take care of the family's financial needs. When children are starting to learn the Qur'an at the age of five and up, the father begins to share with the mother in the activities of parenting. As children grow older, fathers deal mostly with their sons while the mothers are in charge of their daughters. Because of these differentiated roles in the parenting of Somali children, mothers are less skilled at teaching their older sons. In the same way, fathers are less equipped to raise their daughters.

On the other hand, the Islamic faith mandates men to be responsible for their wives, mothers, sisters, and daughters. The traditional roles of mothers and fathers in Muslim/Somali families aid the learning of Islamic values that build the personality of the children. These values are essential in and preparing the children for religious family and community responsibilities.

While in the refugee camps, parents became preoccupied with survival over anything else, if they were lucky enough to be together with their children in the camps. Because of the refugee culture and the stresses on Somali families in Minnesota, the benefits of the traditional Islamic upbringing are sometimes missing.

Some teenage boys, who have been raised by normal Somali cultural standards, try to take the responsibility of the father and the big brother. They are responsible and they listen, respect, and obey their mothers. Others, who lack proper parenting, abuse the role that males have in the Somali culture and expose that new culture to schools. They also rush to learn American culture, but learn the negative aspects first. These teenage boys might frustrate female teachers who do not understand how to handle them.

Handling the new behaviors of these teenagers is a new experience even for Somali men. However, the best model that worked best and that we have applied in our schools is that male relatives as well as mothers be invited into schools. They may become involved when boys refuse to take directions from the female teachers and, together with the teacher, have conferences where a monitoring plan is developed. Using bilingual male staff is also another strategy to use especially when the option of the male relative is missing.

Vignette 5: Spanking

With the help of bilingual staff members, Mr. Sato was very good about keeping in contact with the parents of his students. When one of them did something exceptionally well, parents received a phone call. Parents also received calls when his students did something that they should not have.

Basra had trouble keeping her hands to herself. Sometimes she would "borrow" things from other students without asking. She was also occasionally guilty of name-calling. She also to loved getting conflicts started between students, and then standing back to watch the results.

What amazed Mr. Sato was that whenever he called Basra's mother, Basra would come to school the next day completely contrite. There were also times when Mr. Sato would just make the suggestion to Basra that he was going to make a phone call home, and Basra would become uncharacteristically compliant.

Mr. Sato wanted to know what Basra's mother was doing at home to influence Basara's behavior at school. At parent conferences, Mr. Sato went out on a limb and asked her. Basara's mother became serious, and quiet. She seemed unwilling to answer the question.

Explanation: Spanking is a common form of punishment in the Somali community. Perhaps Basara's mother did not want to answer Mr. Sato's question because there is a common misconception in the Somali refugee community that spanking is illegal in the United States. There is the belief that if a parent is caught spanking a child, the government will intervene and take the child away (Yusef, 2001). In some very unfortunate situations, children have used their parents' fear of losing their children by threatening to call Health and Human Services to report abuse when in fact there was no abuse.

It is important for Somali parents to learn that legal codes in the United States distinguish between corporal punishment and child abuse. This may be difficult to communicate because it is an extremely contentious issue in American society. To many, the difference between spanking and a beating is simply a matter of degree. This is a sensitive area where bilingual staff in the school system should be trained to help parents understand what their rights and responsibilities are under the law.

Vignette 6: Rural vs. Urban

Omar and Awali arrived at the school on the same day. Ms. Kelly seated the two boys together and assumed that they would become friends and help each other through the transition. She also assumed that they would be very similar in their levels of previous exposure to school, and would need the same kind of attention to give them a successful start. Within a few days, however, Ms. Kelly learned that the boys would not easily become friends. Instead, they fought constantly.

As Ms. Kelly started to get to know the boys better she learned that they were actually very different. Omar caught on quickly to the routines of school, and seemed to learn reading and writing in English very quickly. Awali struggled with writing his name. Omar seemed to know a lot about way things worked, but new things constantly surprised Awali. In fact, Ms. Kelly was amazed to find out that Awali had never ridden a bicycle. Ms. Kelly still was not sure why the boys fought all of the time. There was obviously something that she did not understand.

Explanation: Teachers who make the assumption that all Somali kids have everything in common are assuming too much. Like most Somalis, Awali may have come from a rural, nomadic life where survival depended on the health of animal herds, and perhaps Omar came to Minnesota from an urban middle- or upper-middle-class background.

Also, the civil war was a contest between various clans and ethnic groups, and the animosity between them has not completely healed. As conflicts arise between Somali students in the classroom, it is important for teachers to learn as much about the backgrounds of their individual students as possible in order to help in coping with and resolving conflicts.

Vignette 7: "Give me that!"

Fawzia and Amal sat next to each other in Ms. Hays' class. Everything was going ever so well, until Fawzia blurted out, "Give me that! Ms. Hays, tell her to give me my pencil!"

The first time this happened, Ms. Hays went to the girls, identified the pencil in question, and returned it to its rightful owner. The next time it happened, however, Amal denied that she had taken anything. The problem was a lot more difficult to resolve.

Ms. Hays started to watch Amal closely. She noticed that Amal would often take things that did not belong to her. She would just reach out and grab what she wanted. Ms. Hays also noticed that Amal did not take out of need. She had a bundle of pencils, four inches thick, hidden away in her backpack.

Amal carried her backpack with her everywhere. If Ms. Smith required her to leave her backpack in the room, Amal protested, demanding that she take her backpack with her. She was afraid that someone would steal from her.

Explanation: Private property is fairly new concept to previously nomadic people. In Somalia, if someone had a need to use something, he could take it and return it later. Communal property is a necessity to the nomadic lifestyle so that people would not need to carry things that they could borrow. In the United States borrowing without asking first is viewed as stealing. Teachers may need to explicitly teach students to ask politely before taking things. One teacher even carried candy in his pocket to reward students whom he witnessed asking politely and saying "thank you."

Amal hoarded pencils in her backpack. She was so protective of her pencils that she was afraid that if she left them alone, someone else would take them from her. It is entirely speculation, but this behavior may come from the scarcity she experienced early in her life. In any case, it is imperative to gain the trust of students so that the teacher can play the role of mediator in such disputes.

Vignette 8: Boys Disrespecting Girls

Mr. Holdt had taught high school ESL for many years and had worked with kids from many different cultural backgrounds, but he had never taught Somali students before. For the most part, everything was going very well for his Somali students, except for Khalid. Khalid used inappropriate language, and he could not keep his hands to himself. Mr. Holdt did not know what Khalid was saying, but he knew that he was being very insulting and abusive toward the Somali girls in the class. One day Khalid made some comments in Somali to a Somali girl in the class, and put his hand on her head. Mr. Holdt admonished Khalid to keep his hands to himself, and wrote a discipline referral and sent Kahlid to I.S.S. (In-School Suspension).

Before Kahlid left the room, he said, to Mr. Holdt, "So what? She's going to be touched anyway!" Later, when Mr. Holdt told Kahlid that he must be more respectful to the girls in class, Kahlid told Mr. Holdt that it was a cultural difference.

Explanation: Outside of speculation, it is impossible to say why Kahlid behaved the way that he did. Disrespect toward women is not a Somali cultural value. It is possible, however, that Kahlid witnessed extreme cases of violence against women, and has misconstrued violent behavior as normal.

By sending Kahlid to I.S.S. Mr. Holdt was giving the right message, that disrespect and violent behavior toward female classmates is not normal behavior and will not be tolerated. Teachers and administrators need to be firm and consistent in order assure that classrooms are safe places for all students to learn. Other possible interventions could include interviews with bilingual staff, counseling, and therapy.

Vignette 9: Crying

On the first day that Lela came to school she was crying. Every day after that, whenever something surprised her or irritated her, she cried. She also often cried as she waited for the bus to go home. Ms. Thompson, her second-grade teacher, did not know what to do. She watched Lela very carefully to see if she could figure out what she was crying about. She also talked to the bilingual assistant and to Lela's mother, but they did not give her the information she was looking for either.

Ms. Thompson is a very nurturing person, and often hugs and holds her students. Lela needed a lot of that. Sometimes, she could not get Lela to sit down for reading time because Lela was clinging to her.

One day, Ms. Thompson asked the bilingual assistant to accompany her and Lela outside the classroom. She talked to Lela in a calm voice and told her that she was perfectly safe at school, and that nobody was going to come and take her away. She reassured Lela that every day when she came to school, Ms. Thompson would be there to teach her. From that day on, Lela's crying stopped. She embraced school and became one of Ms. Thompson's most engaged students.

Explanation. The Somali children who are coming to American schools have experienced a great deal of upheaval in their lives. The civil war has displaced them and their families from their homes, many of them have experienced violence, physical trauma, malnutrition and the loss of family members and other loved ones, only to be settled in a place that is vastly different from their home. Sometimes they simply need to be assured that they are safe and loved.

It is extremely important to develop personal relationships and trust between teachers and students. A call home about good things that are happening at school can extend that trust and good will toward the family as well.

CHAPTER SIX

Pedagogical Considerations

University programs in teacher education and years of experience have still not taught all of us how to teach and inspire each and every child. However, through our own experiences as teachers of Somali students, and through ideas and suggestions we have collected from others, we have assembled a few insights that may help teachers better serve the needs of their Somali students.

The Need for a Structured Learning Environment

Principals who worked with Ms. McNulty always complimented her on her organization and classroom management skills. She rarely had to redirect off-task behavior because her students always knew what they were supposed to be doing. When Somali students started enrolling in her class, however, she started to doubt her classroom management skills. Her Somali students were talking out in class, walking around the room at inappropriate times, and were constantly interrupting her as she was teaching.

She also noticed, however, that when her Somali students became engrossed in an activity, it was difficult to get them to stop. There were many times when her students were so intensely involved that they would protest when she directed them to make a transition.

Without exception, transition times caused the most trouble. Ms. McNulty used an automotive metaphor to describe the dynamic. As long as their foot was on the gas, the class proceeded smoothly. As soon as they decelerated to make a transition to another activity, the class would slide into disarray. Typically during a transition time, one of her

Somali students would leave her seat to sharpen a pencil or throw something away, and, instead, would start singing or playing loudly with another student. Often accusations of "stealing" a pencil or name-calling would occur during unstructured class time as well.

Explanation.

> Q: Put a hundred kids in a room. How do you know which one is Somali?

> A: Tell them all to sit down. The last one may happen to be Somali.

Besides language barriers, many Somali students entered school at a late age and have not learned the classroom behaviors that we take for granted. Also, children raised in chaotic situations may show their worst behavior when the lessons and classroom environment are disorderly (Psycher, 2001). Classroom procedures need to be explicitly taught and routinely reinforced. Sitting down at the beginning of class, hand raising, turn taking, and not interrupting others are all learned classroom behaviors.

Classroom behavior expectations are part of our peculiar school culture. Teachers are advised to post rules and expectations in a visible place. The rules should be very clearly written, explicitly understood, and should become a matter of routine. If there is a need to call home, it is not enough for a parent to be told that the child is misbehaving in school. It is important to also communicate behavior expectations and consequences to parents, so that parents will clearly understand what the call is for.

Be reminded that Somali students come from a more strict discipline environment than do most of their American classmates. Some of their misbehaviors may come from following the lead of classmates. It is important that discipline is administered fairly and consistently (Psycher, 2001).

Skill Deficits and Academic Assets

Many of the Somali newcomers have come from a nomadic background, where schooling was not necessary, or where schooling was interrupted by the civil war. As a result, many of these students come to us with pre-emergent or undeveloped literacy skills. In fact, Somali students who are as old as sixth and seventh grade may still be struggling with handwriting. Because of a lack of early school experience, the small hand muscles required for intricate tasks are often underdeveloped (Runchy, 1999).

On the other hand, Somali students who come from a cultural background so rich in the oral tradition may have memorization and oral competencies that cannot be measured by tests of reading and writing. Poets are held in high esteem. As a result of this tradition, many Somali students have an ability and willingness to memorize material. This can be a useful tool in helping children learn (Runchy, 1999). Perhaps the concept of literacy is too narrowly defined in schools. Much of the best-known Somali literature has only recently been written down. Masny (1999) points out that a "broader view of literacy," wide enough to include the oral tradition is in order: "ultiple and competing literacy practices point to notion that *becoming literate has more to do with reading the world than reading the word*" (p. 90).

Several teachers who work with Somali students have reported that Somali children love homework. For beginning writers, the act of creating a written piece is very pleasing. When homework is sent home, entire families have sometimes pitched in to help. One teacher sent home an assignment in a workbook with a Somali child, only to have the entire book finished by others in the family learning English (Runchy, 1999). Another teacher, who went to a Somali home to tutor a student individually, reported that after she had begun to read a story to the child, the entire family, including aunts and uncles, circled around her on the floor to listen to the story. When she was finished, everyone applauded!

Independent vs. Cooperative Work

Mr. Lee was doing his best to understand his Somali students. However, his Somali students seemed to have having trouble with critical thinking skills and working independently. In other words, when he asked students to work independently, they seemed driven to collaborate. For example, he struggled to get them to read a book quietly for 15 minutes. His Somali students also insisted on his help when he would give them tasks that required that they make inferences or draw their own conclusions. When he refused, they often protested that since they did not know the answer, they needed him to give it to them.

Explanation: It is important to recognize that Somalis are gregarious, social people. Their communities are extremely interactive and interdependent. Especially in nomadic cultures, interdependence is the key to survival. Simply stated, Somali students will benefit from activities that are collaborative, but they may also need a great deal of guidance with independent learning activities.

The interdependence of Somali life, combined with survival skills honed through the refugee experience, make the difference between cheating and cooperation a difficult lesson for many Somali students to learn. Especially at the secondary level, the difference between cheating and cooperation needs to be taught explicitly. Students may otherwise view sharing answers on a test or copying homework as an acceptable survival skill (Psycher, 2001).

It is also important to remember that "critical thinking skills" are valued more in societies where independence and individualism are also considered important. Individualistic behavior is not affirmed in all cultures. The Somali concept of education stresses memorization and recitation. As a result, Somali students tend to be concrete thinkers, so abstract concepts may be challenging to them. Also, the collective nature of Somali communities de-emphasizes individual responsibility. Most Somali students will need practice working independently.

CHAPTER SEVEN

Conclusion

Teachers and administrators who work with Somali students have more questions than answers. Many of those questions they may try to answer themselves through incomplete knowledge of Somali culture and Islamic tradition. We believe that this method of working through and understanding cultural differences can lead teachers to come up with a variety of misconceptions about their students. When we lack knowledge about others, we tend to invent it. Without a basic foundation of information for teachers about who their Somali students are, a prevailing "conventional wisdom" can develop. We hope that by answering this question, "What information will help public school teachers and administrators accommodate and educate Somali students?" we have provided an accurate foundation of information that will help teachers and administrators become engaged in the process of discovering who their Somali students are.

In the decades to come, the level of cultural diversity in the United States will continue to rise. As teachers, we need to broaden our points of view and seek to learn about the cultures of our students. As we learn, it becomes our responsibility to change the institutions where we work. Teaching refugee children who have come from cultures that are vastly different than our own is only part of the immense challenge we are facing. Each of us needs to answer of whether we will resist the change, or whether we will help to shape the change for a better future for our students.

Many people who have not had significant contact with people from another culture live in a "single context" world (Hall, 1989). They may operate under the ideal that everybody is basically the same, and that they should not draw attention to differences of any kind. In our increasingly diverse schools, we cannot afford to create an atmosphere where the dominant culture becomes the accepted status quo, rejecting other cultural points of view. Only by growth in awareness of our own cultures, the incorporation of a wide variety of cultural elements into curricula, providing a variety of role models to our students, and by helping parents to understand and get involved in the education of their children, will we be able to help all of our students achieve their potential (Delpit, 1988).

We harbor no hope that this handbook has answered all of the questions that teachers will have about their Somali students. In fact, if our work has stimulated as many questions than it has answered, we have done part of what we set out to do. Our handbook is only meant to be a starting point for understanding Somali and Islamic culture. We hope that this book will help educators with the first story of scaffolding they need in their journey toward a better understanding of their Somali students and families.

FOLLOW-UP QUESTIONS AND ACTIVITIES

Chapter One: A Sketch of Islamic and Somali Culture

Values, Values (What they are not)

1. What similarities do you see between basic Islamic values and those held by other religious groups of which you are familiar? In your group, or with a partner, make a Venn diagram comparing and contrasting the Islamic values outlined in this segment with Christianity, Judaism, or Buddhism.

2. In light of terrorist attacks worldwide and those perpetrated against the United States, many people in American society do not consciously separate those who practice Islam from Islamic extremists whom they hear about through the media. Discuss with a partner or with a group how you would address the problem of Muslim students at your school being singled out or harassed because of their Islamic heritage and practice.

3. Muslims put an extremely high value on charity. Discuss in your groups the possibility of organizing a service project with your class or in your school. What connections could you make with the Islamic community in your school to include them in such a project?

4. The issues of collective identity, respect for adults, education, and parental involvement were also discussed in this segment. In small groups or pairs, make a brief list of questions that the discussion of these issues raised, or surprises.

5. In the segment about language, Somalia's rich oral tradition was mentioned. What implications do you see for enriching the educational experience of children who are being raised in an oral tradition? What benefits are there for teachers and staff members learning simple greetings and some other basic vocabulary in their students' native languages?

Islamic Festivals and Holidays

How important is it for teachers to be aware of the holidays celebrated by their students' families?

1. How can you and the rest of the staff in your building promote respect and understanding of holidays and celebrations of all of the

families represented in your school community, even though only the traditional Christian and American holidays are represented on the school calendar?

2. Is it important to provide equal respect and recognition for all holidays and celebrations, or is it better not to discuss religious underpinnings, and only focus discussion on secular dates?

3. How is it possible to communicate honor and respect for cultures other than you own that goes beyond the recognition of holidays?

Family Gender Roles

In much of Western society, a heated debate over the role of women has been ongoing for the past 50 years. As a result, a huge cultural shift has taken place where women today have more opportunities and more choices than they did 50 years ago. In small groups or in pairs, create two Venn diagrams. In the first, compare the role of women in American society 50 years ago with the role of women in American society today. In the second Venn diagram, compare what you know about the role or women in Somali society with the role of women in American society today. Discuss the results of this exercise with the class.

1. Reread the following statement: "*Although many Western readers may find these traditional Islamic arrangement outdated or unsatisfactory, it is important to remember that to Somalis who are not living among Westerners, a more "liberated" point of view is irrelevant.*" Do you agree or disagree? Why?

2. Review some of the problems that might arise for a Somali widow who is raising children in Minnesota.

Educational System

1. How might the teaching methods that you employ be viewed by someone who was educated in Somalia?

2. In pairs or in your group, make a list of the basic school-wide and classroom expectations that are regularly communicated to students. What special efforts do you or could you make to communicate those expectations to students and parents who are not familiar with the American school system?

3. Are there expectations that you have of students that you feel are so basic that you take them for granted, and thus you don't explicitly communicate them? What are they? Are there some that should be clearly communicated to second language learners and their families?

4. Imagine what the expectations might be in a Somali school? In what way are those expectations different from the expectations at your school? Develop methods in which the teachers and administrators can effectively communicate the school expectations.

Chapter Two: A Brief History of Somalia
Why Minnesota?

1. Look up a time line of the Somali civil war. Figure out the age that your students were when some of these events were taking place. Why is this information important to the task of educating your Somali students?

2. Someone says to you, "I don't know why all of these Somalis chose to come to Minnesota. Why didn't they go someplace more like their home?" Develop a response.

3. Clan identity is historically and culturally important to Somalis. Why is it a sensitive issue, and almost never talked about in Minnesota or elsewhere in the Diaspora?

Chapter Three: The Stress on Somali Families in Minnesota

1. In an average American middle-class household, parenting can be very stressful. What are some of the additional stresses experienced by Somali newcomers and their families?

2. Describe with a partner or members of your group some connections that this chapter has helped you make to individual Somali students and their families? What similar stresses have other refugee groups in Minnesota schools experienced? What stresses seem unique to Somali families?

Chapter Four: Accommodating Somali Students in Public Schools
Getting Oriented

1. Develop strategies for welcoming new Somali students to your school. Who should greet them when they come into the building? What information should be made available to them? How should it be communicated?

2. Create a lesson plan for secondary students that would provide those who have negative feelings toward their new life in the United States for an outlet for expressing those feelings constructively.

A Simple Handshake

1. Generally speaking, greetings in American culture are informal. People commonly make direct eye contact, shake hands, refer to each other by first name, and occasionally exchange a touch on the shoulder or elbow. How could members of other cultures misinterpret this informal style? In what ways could a teacher use these differences in the classroom to teach about differences in cultural communication styles?

2. A male teacher or principal on your staff approaches a Somali mother with an outstretched hand. He also occasionally touches female students on the shoulder as a gesture of affection. What do you say to him?

Names

1. In the vignette, Mr. Cornel made a false assumption about his student based on the difference between her name and her mother's name. What could be the long-term implications of his mistake?

2. What other problems could arise form the lack of birth certificates and other written records? Are you aware of other systems for naming children? What cultures use those systems? What does the Somali system for naming children teach us about Somali culture? How could naming systems be integrated into a lesson?

Pork

1. What accommodation has the food service in your school or district made for students who cannot eat pork?

2. What can be done in your school to better train food service personnel and students about which foods contain pork?

3. Imagine that you are going on a class picnic with a class of students, many of whom are Muslim. The student counsel has voted to have bratwurst on the picnic. What alternative would you plan?

Prayer

1. Accommodating Muslim students during prayer times is perhaps the most visible challenge that schools have had to make because of rigid schedules and lack of space. Discuss the situation at your school. How has your staff and administration addressed this issue? What problems have arisen? What creative solutions do you have that haven't been tried yet

2. How do you respond to the following concern: "In public schools, they don't let Christians pray. I don't understand why we have to help Muslim kids pray in school."

Fasting

1. Aside from the lunch routine, what are some of the educational implications of students fasting during the holy month of Ramadan? In what ways can schools demonstrate to Somali parents that Muslim religious practices are recognized and respected, without directly teaching those practices on school property?

Physical Education

1. In your school, what accommodations are made for Muslim students in physical education classes?

2. Whose responsibility is it to be sure that Muslim students are enrolled in alternative classes and that physical education teachers are educated about Islamic dress codes and restrictions?

3. What alternatives could be offered to Islamic students who do not participate in physical education?

4. How important is it for Somali parents to be informed about the contents of the physical education curriculum?

Music Class

1. How can teachers find out from parents what their individual views are on music class?

2. Which students may participate and which ones may not? What practical alternatives could be made available to students at your school whose parents prefer them not to participate in music?

Using a Song in a Lesson

1. How do you respond to a student who says, "we're not supposed to listen to music?"

2. How might you explain to a parent the educational value of music in the classroom?

Art Class

1. Make a list of the lessons that you have done with students, or that you have seen done, that require students to draw people or animals. What are some alternatives that could be offered to students who are not allowed to create images of animals or people?

Health Class

1. How can a health teacher accommodate for Muslim students during discussions of sex and sexuality without singling them out or embarrassing them?

Dating

1. Compare the courtship tradition that your were raised in to one that is very different from yours? What difficulties might Somali adolescents have in an American middle or high school? What pressures do they face?

Clothes

1. Create a lesson that is designed to teach students the significance of the hejab in Islamic cultures. What steps could be taken on a school-wide basis to educate students in the general population and other teachers about Islamic dress codes?

Halloween

1. What other holidays might Islamic parents object to being taught to their children?

2. How can we teach about holidays and traditions without creating an environment of exclusion in the classroom?

Homework

1. Create a system for your classroom whereby parents who do not speak English and may not understand the curriculum can become involved in their children's homework.

Race

1. Imagine that a child has recently arrived in the United States and has only seen white people in magazines. What cultural background information do you take for granted that this student would need to understand before beginning a unit on some aspect of African American history?

2. How might new Somali immigrants process the experience of discrimination differently than a person of color who was born in the United States?

Gestures

1. Did any of the gestures listed in this section surprise you?

2. Tell your partner about a time when you made one of these gestures and how your intent was possibly misinterpreted.

Bibliography

Ahmed, N. (1969). *The fundamental teachings of Quran and Hadith.* N. Ahmed (Ed.), Karachi: Jamiyatul Falah Publications.

Ali, H. (1998, March). Somali women's group. International Institute of Boston and Tufts University (sponsors), *Women in War Conference.* Testimony distributed on a fact sheet by the International Institute of Boston.

Arnaz, D. (1952). Lucy is enciente (J. Oppenheimer, producer). *I Love Lucy.* New York: DesiLu Productions.

Berns McGown, R. (1999). *Muslims in the Diaspora: The Somali communities of London and Toronto.* Toronto, Ont: University of Toronto Press.

Bijelic, M. (1998). Refugee youth: School considerations. *Working Effectively with Schools to Address the Needs of Refugee Children.* Unpublished symposium notes, The Center for Victims of Torture, Minneapolis, MN.

Burton, R. (1966). *First footsteps in East Africa.* In G. Waterfield (Ed.), New York: Prager. (Original work published 1856.)

The Center for Victims of Torture (2000). *Torture and war trauma: Information for refugee communities* [brochure].

Clarke, J. (2000). *Everest to Arabia.* Calgary, Alta: Azimuth.

Cummins, J. (1986). Empowering minority students: A framework for intervention. *Harvard Educational Review.* 56(1), 18-36.

Delpit, L. (1995). *Other people's children: Cultural conflict in the classroom.* New York: W.W. Norton & Company, Inc.

Dini, S. (2001, May). Somali culture; Overview and families. In Community University Health Center (CUHCC) and The Center for Victims of

Torture (sponsors), *Somali Culture and Mental Health*. Symposium providing training for American Human Service Workers, Minneapolis, MN.

Edwards, V. B. (Ed.). (2000). *Lessons of a century: A nation's schools come of age*. Bethesda, MD: Educational Projects in Education.

Hall, E.T. (1989). *Beyond culture*. New York, NY: Anchor Books.

Huber T., Heigher, S., & Pascal, (1992). Case studies in culturally responsive pedagogy. *Mid-Western Educational Researcher*, 5, 9-14.

Husein, I. (1997). *Teenage refugees from Somalia speak out*. New York: The Rosen Publishing Group, Inc.

Husen, A. (2001, May). History of Somalia: Resettlement issues/acculturation. In Community University Health Center (CUHCC) and The Center for Victims of Torture (sponsors), *Somali culture and mental health*. Symposium providing training for American Human Service Workers, Minneapolis , MN.

Information Services of the Somali Government (1962). *The Somali peninsula*. Mogadiscio: The Government of the Somali Republic: Author.

Iszatt, J. & Price, R. (1984). Working with children from refugee communities. *Educational and Child Psychology*, 12(3), 52-56.

Kahin, M.H. (1997). *Educating Somali children in Britain*. Stoke on Trent, England: Trentham Books Limited.

Liebkind, K., & Jasinskaja-Lahti, I. (2000). Acculturation and psychological well-being among immigrant adolescents in Finland: A comparative study of adolescents from different cultural backgrounds. *Journal of Adolescent Research*, 15(4), 446-469.

Masny, D. (1999) Weaving multiple literacies: Somali children and their teachers in the context of school culture. *Language, Culture and Curriculum*. 12, 72-93

Mohamud, H. (2001, May). Muslim faith as it relates to mental health. In Community University Health Center (CUHCC) and The Center for Victims of Torture (sponsors), *Somali Culture and Mental Health*. Symposium providing training for American Human Service Workers, Minneapolis, MN.

Nelson, T. (2000, September 24) They just want some peace. *Saint Paul Pioneer Press*. Pp. 1B, 6B.

Nieto, S. (1999). *The light in their eyes: Creating multicultural learning communities*. New York: Teachers College Press.

Nuruddin, F. (2000). *Yesterday, tomorrow: Voices from the Somali diaspora*. New York: Cassel.

Psycher, T. (2001, May). Classroom management strategies that work. The Center for Victims of Torture (sponsor), *Addressing the Needs of Refugee Youth*. Symposium providing training for school staff, Minneapolis, MN.

Putman, D.B., & Noor, M.C. (1993). *The Somalis: Their history and culture*. Refugee Service Center, Center for Applied Linguistics CAL Refugee Fact sheet No. 9 Washington DC.

Runchey, K. (1999, Winter). Working with Somali students. Articles from the *MinneTESOL Newsletter*. [on-line] http://www.users.uswest.net/~lindaleb/

Reabe, R. (2001, May 8). Live from Steele County Administration Center in Owatonna. *Mainstreet Remote Broadcast*. Saint Paul, MN: Minnesota Public Radio.

Safer, M. (narrator, producer) (1985). *60 Minutes* (television series) ""The Wausau Story." New York: Colombia Broadcasting Corporation.

Scott, S. (2001, May 26). The truth about Islam. *Saint Paul Pioneer Press*. Pp.10E, 5,E.

Refugee Service Center (1999). Refugee Fact Sheet No. 9: *Somalis: Their history and culture*. Washington, DC: [on-line] http://www.cal.org/rsc/Somali/speop.html

Takaki, R. (1993). *A different mirror: A history of multicultural America*. New York: Little, Brown and Company.

Tolan, P. (1997). *Secrets and Ellen* (Gil Junger, Director) Ellen. Los Angeles, CA: ABC Productions.

United States Census Bureau (1990). *Language use and English ability, persons 5 years and over, by state* [electronic data table]. United States Census Bureau [producer and distributor]. http://www.census.gov/population/socdemo/language/table1.txt

U.S. Department of State (1998). *Background notes, Somalia*. Washington DC: [on-line] www.state.gov/www/background_notes/Somalia_0798_bgn.html

Victorian Foundation for Survivors of Torture Inc. (1996). *Guide to working with young people who are refugees*, Used in Minnesota schools project training, The Center for Victims of Torture, Minneapolis, MN.

Williams, S.T. (2001, February 12). For Somali refugees, mental illness often a wordless struggle. *Minneapolis Star Tribune*. Pp. A1, A7.

Yusuf, A. (2001, May). Somali culture: Children/youth. In Community University Health Center (CUHCC) and The Center for Victims of Torture (sponsors), *Somali culture and mental health*. Symposium providing training for American Human Service Workers, Minneapolis, MN.